Teaching Through Texts

Using a wide range of genres including poetry, playscripts, picture-books, performance texts, comics, classics, cinema texts, novels, non-fiction and pupils' own narratives, this book seeks to show how texts can be used to make literacy exciting and pleasurable in the primary classroom.

Drawing on many popular as well as literary texts the contributors write with enthusiasm about opportunities for creative teaching and learning. They also provide many examples of good practice to promote literacy, both inside and outside the Literacy Hour.

While *Teaching Through Texts* includes a discussion of the National Literacy Strategy, it also looks ahead to the new literacies of the future.

Holly Anderson is joint Language Co-ordinator at Homerton College, Cambridge. She has many years of experience as a teacher in early years and has published widely in the field. **Morag Styles** is Reader in Children's Literature and Language at Homerton College, Cambridge. She recently published *Opening the Nursery Door* with Routledge.

Teaching Through Texts

Promoting literacy through
popular and literary texts
in the primary classroom

Edited by Holly Anderson
and Morag Styles

London and New York

First published 2000
by Routledge
11 New Fetter Lane, London EC4P 4EE

Simultaneously published in the USA and Canada
by Routledge
29 West 35th Street, New York, NY 10001

Routledge is an imprint of the Taylor & Francis Group

Typeset in Goudy by Florence Production Ltd., Stoodleigh,
Devon
Printed and bound in Great Britain by
Biddles Ltd, Guildford and King's Lynn

British Library Cataloguing in Publication Data
A catalogue record for this book is available
from the British Library

Library of Congress Cataloging in Publication Data
Teaching through texts: promoting literacy through popular and
literary texts in the primary classroom/[edited by] Holly Anderson
and Morag Styles.
     p. cm.
  Includes bibliographical references and index.
  1. Reading (Primary)–Great Britain. 2. Children's literature–
Study and teaching (Primary)–Great Britain. 3. Literacy–Great
Britain. I. Anderson, Holly. II. Styles, Morag.
LB1573.T39 1999
372.64'044'0941–dc21   99–28349
                                                             CIP

ISBN 0 415 20306 6 (hbk)
ISBN 0 415 20307 4 (pbk)

This book is dedicated with affection and respect to the memory of our friend and colleague Helen Arnold

Contents

Figures

Contributors

Holly Anderson is a Language Co-ordinator at Homerton College, Cambridge.

Helen Bromley is a Tutor at the Centre for Language in Primary Education.

Chris Doddington is Senior Lecturer in Drama and Education at Homerton College, Cambridge.

Anne Fine is a prizewinning author of many novels, mostly for children, and has been shortlisted for the Children's Laureate.

Jim Jones is Head of English at Chesterton Community College, Cambridge.

Sarah Jones was Education Officer at the Arts Cinema, Cambridge, and is now a Lecturer at Anglia Polytechnic University.

Andy Kempe is Senior Lecturer in Drama and Education at Reading University.

Mary Purdon is Language Co-ordinator at Longthorpe Primary School, Peterborough.

Kate Rabey teaches reception at Queen Edith's Primary School, Cambridge.

Frances Smith teaches English and Education at Homerton College, Cambridge, and at the Open University.

Vivienne Smith teaches at Worcester College of Education, and is studying for a PhD.

Morag Styles is Reader in Children's Literature and Language at Homerton College, Cambridge.

Isobel Urquhart is a Language Co-ordinator at Homerton College, Cambridge.

Nick Warburton is a well-known writer of fiction and plays, mostly for young people.

Acknowledgements

Extracts from 'Ar-a-Rat' and 'Give Yourself a Hug' by Grace Nichols are reproduced with permission of Curtis Brown Ltd, London, on behalf of Grace Nichols. Copyright Grace Nichols 1991, 1994. 'Ar-a-Rat' was first published in *No Hickory No Dickory No Dock* (Viking, 1991) and 'Give Yourself a Hug' was published in *Give Yourself a Hug* (A. & C. Black, 1994).

Extracts from 'Marty Smarty' by John Foster are reproduced with permission of Oxford University Press, on behalf of John Foster.

Extracts from *The Monster Bed* by Jeanne Willis are reproduced with permission of Andersen Press Ltd, London, on behalf of Jeanne Willis.

Figure 9.1, the packaging for Kellogg's Choco Krispies, appears by kind permission of Kellogg Company.

Figure 9.2, Farmyard Greetings by Rachel O'Neill and N. E. Middleton, is reproduced with permission of Camden Graphics Ltd.

Introduction

Teaching through texts – contexts, conventions and contributors

Morag Styles

In the last fifteen or so years, and regardless of the secretary of state for education in office, we have witnessed in Britain an unprecedented focus of attention on literacy with wave after wave of initiatives from government agencies. In early 1999 the National Literacy Strategy[1] decreed that for one hour each day – the Literacy Hour – every primary school up and down the land will teach reading and writing according to strict and detailed time and content guidelines. There is no legislation in place to make the National Literacy Strategy compulsory, but everyone concerned with the literacy of primary-school children knows that its directives must be followed. Margaret Meek[2] told us many years ago that *we teach what we think reading is*. The autonomy of teachers in respect of what, when, where and how to teach reading has disappeared. Indeed, the Labour Government has to a significant extent staked its credibility on the success of this venture, promising to deliver markedly improved results in Reading and Writing SATs[3] before the next election.

As usual, teachers are in the firing line for what is as much a political as an educational strategy, though the genuine concern of those leading the NLS[4] for improving literacy cannot be doubted. What is deeply frustrating to many practitioners is that research into and classroom evidence of economic factors underlining educational underachievement, such as poverty, racism and problems associated with a growing 'underclass', have been ignored in favour of the panacea that adherence to the NLS is expected to provide. Furthermore, an understanding of literacy as a set of culturally developed practices is singularly lacking from the NLS. Other commentators deplore the exorbitant costs involved in a programme which, on the one hand, has been imposed on teachers and, on the other, has been cobbled together at high speed. That this is the best use of taxpayers' money to promote literacy remains questionable.

Debates about how best to teach reading explode regularly in Britain, and different educational ideologies gain ascendancy at different times. The 1980s and 1990s have been marked by an increasingly traditional and mechanistic view of teaching and learning, whereas the dominant ideology of the 1970s was liberal and, in small but significant quarters, progressive. The major investigation into literacy known as the Bullock Report (1975) seems light years away from the language and values of the NLS. The following extract is typical of the former:

> Controversy about the teaching of reading has a long history, and throughout it there has been the assumption, at least the hope, that a panacea can be found that will make everything right . . . *there is no one method, medium, approach, device or philosophy that holds the key to the process of reading.* We believe that the knowledge does exist to improve the teaching of reading, but that it does not lie in the triumphant discovery, or re-discovery, of a particular formula [emphasis added].[5]

The Bullock Report stresses that no one strategy can be expected to work for the range of difficulties associated with literacy experienced by a small but significant minority of pupils. In contrast, the sometimes uncritical zeal and conformity of those at the centre of this initiative have some of the unhealthy trappings of evangelical movements. Writing before the NLS was even a twinkle in John Stannard's[6] eye, Peter Traves was alert to the differences between what he called 'proper and improper literacy'. His notion of 'improper' literacy could be levelled at the NLS for all its good intentions and (some) good practice: 'the dominance of a particular and . . . mechanistic definition . . . [of literacy, paying] little or no attention to the broad and complex web of behavioural and intellectual patterns that underpin real reading'.[7] Margaret Meek, Hilary Minns, Henrietta Dombey, Myra Barrs and her team at the Centre for Language in Primary Education, each having conducted sustained, detailed, pupil- and teacher-centred research into the learning (and teaching) of reading, have shown us that 'complex web' in action.[8]

   Eve Bearne also has written extensively in this field: in her Postscript to *Greater Expectations* she shows the mistake in the argument that if teachers only got better at teaching by following a particular method or programme, then the standards of children's work in literacy would magically improve.

> Intervention to raise standards of literacy is . . . a highly complex matter . . . not a straightforward link between cause and effect. . . . [R]aising standards of reading and writing means setting up an environment in which learning can be most effective rather than adhering to particular methods or materials. . . .[9]

Using Matthew Arnold's telling metaphor of 'ignorant armies who clash by night' to describe some literacy developments before the advent of the NLS, Eve Bearne underlines the importance of building 'a critical *theory* of literacy in education which . . . is dynamic, recursive and cumulative rather than a linear progress through clearly defined stages . . . [and which] can take into account the cultures of home and school' [emphasis added].[10] Indeed, one of criticisms most often levelled at the NLS is the lack at its heart of a coherent theory.

It is an open secret that one of the reasons behind the Literacy Hour is to combat what has been described as a large tail of reading failure in Britain (i.e. the higher percentage of children here than in Europe who are slow in learning to read). If this statistic is correct (and we remain unconvinced) other factors, such as the age when schooling begins, come into play. At any rate, the Literacy Hour has been imposed on *all* the pupils of England and Wales aged between 5 and 11. What effect it will have on the lowest achievers remains to be seen, but there are worries about boredom, disaffection and underachievement for average and above-average pupils in a curriculum which spends forty minutes of the daily Literacy Hour on whole-class teaching. If these lessons are pitched to the understanding of those who find literacy most challenging, keeping the most academic children involved and interested, day-in, day-out, will be difficult and could prove counterproductive.

Wise teachers will make sensible compromises and adapt the NLS to the needs of their own classes, but the widespread criticism of British schooling in the last ten years by the media, politicians and, most perniciously, a chief inspector of schools who has lost the respect of the majority of teachers, means that many will lack the confidence to deviate from a rigorous programme of literacy teaching. And the hard won right of schools and teachers to have at least the choice of working in mixed-ability settings, has been lost as the Literacy Hour prescribes ability grouping.

Furthermore, the content of the NLS is underscored by what many in the teaching profession have been resisting for years – explicit teaching of extensive rules of grammar, spelling and punctuation, while phonics (rather than the research-based notion of phonological awareness[11]) is privileged as the way to approach reading. Even prime minister Tony Blair exhorts teachers to use phonics more extensively in speeches and interviews! While all those contributing to this book fully support efforts to raise standards in children's abilities to manage the technicalities of language effectively, and while we believe children need to master the basics of punctuation, spelling and grammar in the primary school, the sheer quantity of technical knowledge of language that non-specialist primary teachers and their pupils are expected to master seems to us a serious misjudgement of the strategy.

To make space for the Literacy Hour, the arts curriculum has been sabotaged. How much time and instruction will be spent on painting, drawing and other artistic and creative activities in early years' classrooms of the future, let alone those at the top end of the primary school? The idea of play as the intellectual work of young children which used to be the cornerstone of early years' philosophy is difficult to sustain in a packed and demanding curriculum which includes the reception year. Areas like music, history and geography have already had time (and, in the former case, expertise) decimated.

There is also a serious gap at the centre of the NLS – hardly a mention of visual literacy which, with all the new technologies children are expected to master, will surely be one of the dominant literacies of the twenty-first century. We fail to value the reading of pictures, films, television, CD ROM, performance texts and cartoon strips at our peril. *Teaching Through Texts* gives pictorial literacy the high profile we believe it deserves.

It is the job of those of us who have been in literacy education for some time to take the long-term view and to examine critically all new initiatives, particularly blanket ones, imposed on our pupils and primary teachers. We must rise above fads and factions; we have seen educational initiatives come and go, and we must weigh up each using evidence and experience wisely to enlighten our thinking. As has already been indicated, there are many questions one would wish to raise about the NLS, but now that it is with us, it is only fair to give it a chance, monitoring carefully the most and least effective parts of the strategy. There are also, clearly, some advantages. The greatest of these, it seems to the editors of this book, is putting a wide range of literature at the heart of the Literacy Hour.

Never before have teachers been expected to cover such diverse genres, authors and texts with children. While we have reservations about some of the activities expected of teachers and their pupils at sentence and word level[12] (to use the jargon of the NLS), the guidance materials contain many good ideas which will be helpful to teachers. The emphasis on being explicit about learning purposes and the need to foster closer relationships between reading and writing are positive developments. Perhaps most importantly, working regularly at whole-text level on traditional, 'classic' and modern fiction, non-fiction and poetry can, we believe, do nothing but good. Furthermore, there is embedded an explicit commitment throughout NLS guidance to teaching literature from a wide range of cultures, which is an excellent innovation.

We approve also of the detailed reference to the different sub-genres into which literary genres can be broken, though we recognise that this will be taxing at first for many teachers. The coverage of poetry, for example, is remarkably extensive, and teachers need some reassurance that the categories and technical terms can be quickly mastered, and that some are less important than others. (The difference between concrete and shape poetry, for example, is certainly not something teachers or children should worry about! And the recommendation that children write calligrams at 7 or 8 seems to us unimportant in comparison with getting this age group to enjoy writing poetry and to do so with some confidence.) Although one might quibble with having to teach particular sub-genres at particular times, well-organised teachers will soon accommodate this, and it does have the advantage of avoiding overlap and omission. And, after all, sensible teachers will be flexible – if there are pressing reasons for tackling literature not prescribed for that term, they will cover it, outside of the Literacy Hour if necessary.

While we welcome the full and rich new emphasis on teaching through texts, we also recognise the demands it will make on an already exhausted teaching profession. Change can be only gradual: it takes time to build up a wide repertoire of children's literature, and perhaps even longer to feel confident about using it wisely. The NLS training materials can help, but many teachers will require further support. This is one of the purposes behind this book.

Having worked closely with teachers for many years in training partnerships, and on advanced diplomas and courses relating to professional development,[13] we know that quite a number feel insecure about their own knowledge of children's literature and how best to teach it well at text level. Some will find the tight structure of the Literacy Hour liberating, and it may well improve their practice. Others will find it restrictive. For both groups it is worth remembering that the Literacy Hour is unlikely to survive in its current prescriptive form for very long: it will evolve, as all initiatives do, and probably shake down into something more manageable and flexible. In the meantime, this book aims to serve the interests of inexperienced teachers and trainees who are uncertain how to tackle a wide range of literature in the classroom, working within and without the Literacy Hour format. We aim also to provide inspiration and new ideas, and to indicate a wider than normal range of genres with a strong emphasis on popular culture, for those who are already confident about teaching through texts.

We begin with the centrality of poetry in the early years. In 'Give Yourself a Hug: reading between the rhymes', Vivienne Smith, quoting Margaret Meek, locates early experiences of verse firmly in the home, the community and in children's popular culture: 'Poetry is never better understood than in childhood, when it is felt in the blood and along the bone.'[14] Unlike those who complain that children do not know nursery rhymes these days, Smith believes that such rhymes are embedded in their culture and deeply entrenched in their memories.

Vivienne Smith makes a persuasive case for the way children use rhyme to define themselves as individuals and to bond them to family and community. Her argument takes in the pleasures of nonsense and the affirmative friendship rituals and group oracy of playground rhymes (which she calls winningly the prodigal son of nursery rhyme). Building on this firm foundation, and giving examples from her own early years' classroom, Smith shows how far teachers can take infants in a poetry curriculum which includes Robert Frost, Christina Rossetti and Grace Nichols. She argues that real 'listening skills' are involved in responding to poetry and she shows how the rhythm and music in verse are what first evoke children's response. In an insightful conclusion, Vivienne Smith suggests that poetry helps children to look inwards, developing a relationship with themselves 'to affirm the people they are'.

Helen Bromley also is interested in the popular culture of childhood, but in 'Never be without a *Beano*' her particular focus is comics – how they produce their effects, how sophisticated they are, how they are read by children and where their appeal lies. She demonstrates how the *Beano* provides both predictability and challenge – endearing and subversive characters (just think of Dennis the Menace and Gnasher!), intertextuality, multilayered meanings, self-referential jokes and a wide range of text types, including non-fiction. She shows how the *Beano* respects its readers by making demands on them, while never losing sight of the importance of amusement.

Helen Bromley demonstrates how any issue of the *Beano* provides endless possibilities for work at the word level – there are puns, alliterations, jokes and rhymes aplenty. More challengingly, the *Beano* changes font, print, direction and voice to make subtle points or present ambiguity, such as the 'Notes from the Editor' which to be fully understood require extensive knowledge of different genres. Finally, she shows how comics offer children a wide cultural space in which to locate themselves and how, in turn, far from being flimsy items of popular literature, they are often hoarded and catalogued as well as valued and treasured by their readers.

We move from Dennis the Menace to Minnie the Minx in Chris Doddington's chapter, which looks at the centrality of character in fiction's appeal to young readers. Drawing on diverse characters in children's literature – Little Lord Fauntleroy, Hans Christian Andersen's Little Match Girl, Captain Hook and Roald Dahl's BFG – Chris Doddington shows how young readers learn first to discriminate between heroes and villains, then to appreciate subtler variations. Children begin by identifying with charismatic characters like Max (*Where the Wild Things Are*), George (Blyton), Alice, Huckleberry Finn and Anne of Green Gables, and if exposed to a wide enough range of fiction develop an understanding of the complexity of human beings.

Characterisation is often the hook which draws children into novels, and it is through the actions of characters that they learn about motivation, morality and making mistakes. Taking Kitty from Fine's *Goggle-Eyes* as an example, Chris Doddington considers how a character is gradually built up and slowly revealed in a well-constructed novel through appearance, context, plot, dialogue and interaction with other characters. She goes on to show how the work of some leading educational philosophers can enlighten drama approaches to character. Overall, Chris Doddington's chapter suggests that reading fiction teaches us in a safe way what it means to be human.

Nick Warburton is also interested in characters and their motives and viewpoints, as his chapter focuses on what working on plays can offer young readers. He discusses the importance of giving children opportunities to imagine themselves in other people's shoes; presenting the 'other' by using the self to serve the text can help them to understand themselves, as well as to appreciate what this particular literature offers. Nick Warburton goes on to liken play scripts to musical scores, describing them as sets of instructions; bringing the script to life with its endless possibilities is like reading music.

'When children put on a play, they can cope with texts which are initially perplexing and with language richer and more strange than they are likely to encounter elsewhere.' This is as true when young children read, and especially act, contemporary plays written specially for them, as when tackling Shakespeare and other highly regarded dramatists. But Nick Warburton is concerned also with the non-verbal side of drama, and stresses the role of mime, pauses, movement, gesture and silence alongside issues to do with costume, scenery, lighting and set. Dramatic events and moments of significance are considered in a discussion which looks at different play scripts for stage, film, television and radio for which children can be actors, directors, stage-hands and writers, as well as consumers. Nick Warburton concludes by reflecting on the special kind of writing demanded of play scripts – clear, simple, uncomplicated and with a good sense of audience – and how we can enable children to compose their own versions of these challenging texts.

Andy Kempe's definition of drama is 'the creation and interpretation of visual images'. His chapter shows how drama can be made to work with younger as well as older children, using picture-books as a starting-point. He begins by problematising traditional issue-based improvisation, preferring to focus on symbolism through myth and parable, and drawing on the work of Zipes, Bettelheim and Carter to show how archetypal traditional tales can take on new values and emphases in different times.

Jeanne Willis's *The Monster Bed* proves an excellent vehicle for understanding irony and the contradictions between words and images, and for looking at events from different perspectives with young children. Andy Kempe provides practical ideas for using this text and others like it for drama, which is likened to 'walking in the pages of a book', while offering readers a well theorised justification for his work with children. Finally, he looks at ways of getting underneath stereotypes by activities which involve physicalising dramatic tension, making difficult decisions and dealing with choices. This discussion is informed by a lifetime's experience of teaching drama with different age groups and underpinned by extensive background reading.

Picture books also formed the basis of Mary Purdon's project with pupils aged 5–7, in particular the work of one of Britain's most talented artists, Anthony Browne. She shows how very young children can appreciate colour symbolism, design features and intertextuality in picture books. Finding that her pupils were interested in the artistic conventions employed by Browne, she tried the experiment of inviting an art specialist to teach the children about the surrealism which is prevalent in Browne's work. Her high expectations of the children were realised as they pored over books by Magritte and Dali, side by side with further examination of Browne's texts. Nor was this interest short-lived: the children went on to research the use of Van Gogh and other painters in texts illustrated by Browne.

Mary Purdon carefully observed the children scrutinising Browne's books in order to understand better the nature of his appeal to children. She found their approach to his extensive use of intertextuality a delightful puzzle to solve and a sort of 'deep play'. As she points out, 'they expect to find meaning in every part of a Browne illustration'. So intellectually engaged were the children in reading for every nuance, that they lapped up the technical vocabulary employed to describe visual imagery. Using some of Browne's finest texts, from first to latest publication, Mary Purdon demonstrates how children can interpret the subtle interplay of word and image, understand metaphor and allusion, relate pictures to cultural icons and generally show themselves capable of being sophisticated readers of multilayered illustrated text.

Kate Rabey, who has a fine arts' background herself, similarly focuses on visual literacy in her chapter, which examines two picture-books by the outstanding American authors Lane Smith and Jon Scieszka, *The Stinky Cheese Man* and *The True Story of the Three Little Pigs*, respectively. She is particularly interested in the metafictive nature of these texts and their postmodernist trappings, showing how many of the familiar expectations of storytelling are subverted. Her own interpretations of these texts are enlightening; indeed, she proves that those of us without knowledge of the history of painting are at a disadvantage in reading these books.

Kate Rabey uses examples of children's work in response to *The True Story* to illustrate some of the points she is making. Like Mary Purdon's class, the children found the books engrossing and therefore rose to the challenge of grappling with instability, uncertainty and ambiguity to make meaning. She argues persuasively that reading rich and inventive texts like these is empowering for young readers.

Sarah Jones, who was education officer of the Arts Cinema, Cambridge, at the time of writing, is equally committed to visual literacy, though her focus is reading film. She starts from the position that film is regarded as a weak competitor with the written word in the primary school curriculum, one which when understood as text has huge potential for young readers. Sarah Jones shows how working effectively with film in the classroom requires previewing, specific task-setting and post-screening discussion to begin to unravel its many possibilities. Film has its own language, codes and conventions about which children can enjoy learning.

There are connections with Nick Warburton's chapter, as Sarah Jones is keen to teach children about the technicalities – from understanding and using the practical skills of editing, cutting, montage, camera angle and frame, to design, lighting, music, costume, props, setting and, of course, performance. She goes on to question the predictable view of children as dupes of popular media, seeing them instead as discerning viewers and informed choosers who, far from being passive consumers, understand the messages of the media.

Taking as examples films like *James and the Giant Peach*, *Microcosmos* and *Romeo and Juliet*, Sarah Jones offers practical advice for using these films in the classroom. The differences (where relevant) between film versions of printed text can be interesting for children, but she argues that teachers need to emphasise films as valuable texts in their own right. She does not ignore non-fiction elements of film, such as marketing, posters and sound-track, all of which have classroom potential. Reminding us that in France film education is compulsory, Sarah Jones makes a convincing case for the serious study in the primary school of this versatile genre.

Isobel Urquhart is interested in the texts children compose for themselves. She focuses, in particular, on what pupils with special needs can achieve, collaborating with adults acting as scribes. In a careful analysis of young learners, Isobel Urquhart charts their growing confidence in reading the literature that they have produced for themselves. As well as having a positive benefit on composition and the ability to tackle technical features of language, the psychological rewards of this process in terms of self-esteem and motivation are noted.

Drawing explicitly on Brigid Smith's work in this field, her chapter offers further evidence for what Donald Graves[15] taught us about enabling pupils to be real writers of the texts *they* want to construct which are often rooted in areas of personal expertise, as was the case with Jay and his dictated text about fishing, with which Chapter 10 opens. As well as providing evidence for 'the reader in the writer', Isobel Urquhart's chapter is an uplifting account of how children can learn and teachers teach through pupils' own texts.

Holly Anderson wants children to use structural understanding of texts to facilitate their own reading and writing. In her case the texts are non-fiction: not information books designed specifically for pupils, but the environmental print and artefacts normally found around homes and communities – from cornflake packets and Argos catalogues to birthday cards and party invitations. First of all, Holly Anderson reminds us of the wonderful variety of print and image available which, for some children, form the first 'reading' experiences. She goes on to emphasise how regular literacy events in the home can be exploited in the classroom and how young children can spontaneously produce such texts themselves.

In a practical chapter, Holly Anderson goes on to show the diverse possibilities of working at word, sentence and text levels using travel brochures and the like, focusing on the language used to persuade and sell which is often combined with sophisticated visual features, such as logos, photographs and stunning design imagery. In her final section, Holly Anderson breaks down some of these texts into smaller parts, showing how work on phonological awareness, morphology and metalanguage can naturally flow from studying environmental print in the classroom.

Non-fiction texts are the concern also of Frances Smith – in her case recent information books for children. She begins, however, by reminding us that information-giving is by no means confined to non-fiction and that fiction offers young readers wide possibilities for acquiring knowledge, including an understanding of the human condition: 'It is difficult to disagree with Meek's conviction that issues, moral attitudes and understandings are most effectively presented in novels and picture books.'

Taking as her focus historical information, Frances Smith goes on to consider what happens when we look beneath the surface of the presentation of 'facts' and encounter what Bakhtin[16] called a 'change of speaking subjects' – i.e. exploring some of the different voices involved in the telling, particularly when there are competing viewpoints or ambiguity, even conflict, between them. Her discussion includes texts as varied as *Sophie's World*, *The Dinosaur's Book of Dinosaurs* and *The Blitzed Brits*, and compares different ways of telling from first-person narrative (often fictional) to joky treatment of conventional devices such as autobiography (often invented) and documents (often fake).

Frances Smith invited responses from a group of young readers to her chosen non-fiction texts; their interesting comments show an awareness of the hybrid nature of many information books, and they brought mature understanding to the difficulty of pinning down many 'facts'. The comic treatment of what are actually serious subjects (such as torture in the Elizabethan period) is of dubious taste, and the tension between amusement and instruction is often apparent in these texts. Smith concludes by raising some of the key questions that teachers intend their pupils to apply to information texts.

It was by chance, not design, that many of the contributors to this book chose novels by Anne Fine to exemplify points they wanted to make, though such preference demonstrates the power of Fine's fiction and her position as a leading writer for the young in the late twentieth century. Frances Smith, for example, suggests that Fine is an author who helps readers gain self-knowledge through the plots, characters and issues raised by her novels. Jim Jones agrees with this appraisal, and his chapter provides an appreciation and analysis of what Fine's fiction offers her readers. Also by chance, both Smith and Jones quote the same brief passage from Fine's *Goggle-Eyes* in which her central character states that 'living your life is a long and doggy business. . . . And stories and books help. Some help you with the living itself. Some help you just take a break. . . .'[17]

Jim Jones begins his chapter with the notion of 'taking a break' and highlights the sheer enjoyment and amusement in Fine's novels which allow young readers to take a holiday from 'real life'. He goes on to examine the imaginative inventiveness of her fiction, for younger and older age groups, showing how her books help readers to live that 'long and doggy business'. Jones draws our attention to the fact that most of Fine's prolific *oeuvre* over twenty-five years is based on the realities of home and school life and that she is 'always playing games, but they are serious games'.

Fine's fiction is always grounded in personal growth, though this is often gained by her characters after the struggle in overcoming difficulties. While Jones, like most of Fine's readers, delights in her humour, he also traces the challenging themes with which she tends to deal – how divorce affects children; how it feels for children when parents find new partners; the problems that arise when old, young and middle-aged live together; bullying and abuse. Jim Jones notices how central the act of storytelling is in most of Fine's work; as he puts it, she both demonstrates and advocates the power of narrative.

It was a huge bonus that Anne Fine agreed to write a response to Jim Jones' chapter. She gives us some insights into the highs and lows of writing, the inevitable loneliness of the act itself, and the need to believe that the struggle to make art out of life through the medium of words is worth doing.

> Is this really how I ought to be spending my one life on the planet? . . . I had only just begun to wonder if locking myself away in absolute silence for months on end is really the way I want to live my life. . . . [W]hat is made clear by Jim Jones' study is that the value of writing is something I have been querying all along. . . . [T]he answer I have come to consistently, through so many of my characters, is: Yes. It *is* worth it. Carry on.

Fine reminds us of the rich variety, vitality and vigour of language, form, ideas and themes in contemporary literature for the young. Sharing such texts with children can be one of the greatest joys in primary education. Helping children compose their own texts, which are hugely influenced by the texts they read and hear, valuing these texts and offering a wide audience for them, will promote and develop *critical* literacy in our pupils, who need to be confident in the new literacies of tomorrow.

We began by asking questions and outlining reservations expressed about recent literacy initiatives in Britain. We conclude on a positive note of belief in the best offices of teachers and pupils to grapple with the challenges of literacies, old and new, invigorated and inspired by the work of authors, illustrators, playwrights, film-makers, animators and other talented creators of texts. We hope that the ideas, enthusiasm and professionalism of the contributors to this book will enable readers to discover or extend the value of teaching through texts.

Notes

1 John Major's Conservative Government set up a National Literacy Pilot Scheme in 1997 through which subsequently the principles and philosophy of the Labour Government's National Literacy Strategy have been worked out.

2 Margaret Meek first used this idea in Meek, M. *et al.* (1983) *Achieving Literacy*, London: Routledge.

3 Standardised Attainment Tests (SATs) in Reading and Writing administered annually to all 7- and 11-year-olds in Britain. The results are published on a school-by-school basis.

4 The National Literacy Strategy, hereafter called the NLS, was imposed on all primary schools in England and Wales from September 1998.

5 Department of Education and Science (1975) *A Language For Life* (chair: Sir Alan Bullock), London: HMSO, pp. 77f.

6 John Stannard is director and a key architect of the NLS.

7 Traves, P. (1992) 'Reading: the entitlement to be properly literate', in K. Kimberly, M. Meek and J. Mills (eds) *New Readings: Contributions to an Understanding of Literacy*, London: A. & C. Black.

8 See, for example, Minns, H. (1998) *Read It to Me Now!*, Milton Keynes: Open University Press; Dombey, H. *et al.* (1998) *Whole to Part Phonics*, London: CLPE; Barrs, M. *et al.* (1988) *The Primary Language Record*, London: CLPE (and numerous other publications); Meek *et al.*, *Achieving Literacy*, op. cit.

9 Bearne, E. (1995) *Greater Expectations: Children Reading Writing*, London: Cassell, pp. 211–12.

10 Bearne, E. (1996) 'Mind the gap', in M. Styles, E. Bearne and V. Watson (eds), *Voices Off*, London: Cassell, pp. 311 and 327.

11 See, for example, Goswami, U. and Bryant, P. (1990) *Phonological Awareness and Learning to Read*, London: Lawrence Erlbaum Associates.

12 Text, sentence and word levels relate roughly, in turn, to whole-text issues (genre, setting, character, language), grammar and punctuation matters, and spelling and phonic rules. The language of the document is interesting: whole-text knowledge is categorised as 'comprehension' with all the connotations of old fashioned exercises, whereas many of the activities suggested under this heading are interesting and worthwhile.

13 Continual professional development or in-service training, in Britain currently known as CPD.

14 Meek, M. (1991) *On Being Literate*, London: Bodley Head, pp. 182f.

15 Graves, D. (1983) *Writing: Teachers and Children at Work*, London: Heinemann.

16 Bakhtin, M. (1981) 'Discourse in the novel', in M. Holquist (ed.), *The Dialogical Imagination* Austin, TX: University of Texas Press.

17 Fine, A. (1989) *Goggle-Eyes*, London: Penguin Books, p. 139.

Chapter 1

Give Yourself a Hug

Reading between the rhymes

Vivienne Smith

> Poetry is never better understood than in childhood, when it is felt in the blood and along the bone.
>
> (Meek 1991: 182)

One, two, three, four,
Put your bottom on the floor.
Five, six, seven, eight,
Cross your legs and sit up straight.
Are you ready? Nine, ten:
I've lost the register again!

So, with rhyme and an admission of inadequacy, the day in my reception/ year 1 classroom would begin; and the children thought it was wonderful. They would stop their chatter, sit down, bristle with straightness and chant the rhyme with an enthusiasm and volubility that was sometimes difficult for me to share first thing in the morning.

Our rhyme is nothing special. I include it here because it illustrates the central importance that poetry of all sorts came to have in our classroom. This rhyme, for us and about us, celebrated the delight we found in each other, in rhythm and in language. It was an expression of our community.

This chapter sets out to describe how this sense of community came about. It will consider the work we did in the classroom, but it must begin before that. For most children know poetry from the cradle. It lives and grows with them throughout babyhood and through the pre-school years. Mostly, they know it in the form of nursery rhyme.

In the nursery

One day, in a spare ten minutes, I asked the children in my class to tell me all the nursery rhymes they knew, and we made a list. We were short of time, so the list was not exhaustive, but it contained thirty-five or so songs and rhymes with which the children were familiar. The list contained some texts that I would not call nursery rhymes: *The Wheels on the Bus Go Round and Round* was there and so was the Ahlbergs' *Each Peach Pear Plum*. It seemed that for these children a 'nursery rhyme' was any text that was rhythmic enough to be sung or chanted, was easy to remember and was (probably) associated with the time before they started school.

They showed great enthusiasm for the task: they vied with one another to be first to mention the really well-known rhymes; they exclaimed with delighted recognition when anyone volunteered a rhyme they knew but had forgotten; and they giggled with joy when they found one I did not know.

The rhymes were special to these children. They told me eagerly about the contexts in which they knew them best. 'My mum sings that to me,' said one. 'We used to sing that at playgroup!' 'That's on my tape!' Kitty and Daisy, identical twins, became most excited by two of the rhymes. 'That's mine!' shouted Kitty when we remembered *Humpty Dumpty*. 'It's on my cup. Daisy has got *Jack and Jill*.' The children were surrounded by rhymes. They heard them on tapes, watched them on videos and saw them on the television. Nursery rhymes, or the characters from them, were depicted on cups, on curtains, on toys and in books. The adult-controlled culture in which small children live their daily lives is thick with nursery rhymes and with reference to them.

I asked the children how they first came to know these rhymes, but they could not tell me. For each of them, some rhymes were so deeply entrenched in memory that they could not remember a time when the rhymes were unfamiliar. The learning of them, it seems, had taken place in such a way or at such a time that no effort of conscious recall was needed.

Their mothers confirmed this impression. They told me how they had used rhyme most often when their children had been babies and toddlers. They had sung rhymes and lullabies to rock and soothe the children to sleep. They had amused them and distracted them with finger rhymes and bouncing games. *Pat-a-Cake, Pat-a-Cake, Baker's Man* was mentioned, and so was *This is the Way the Ladies Ride*. Physical contact and rhythmic move-ment were usually part of the experience. These were not occasions of planned cultural induction. Rather they were impromptu moments of fun and tenderness between mother and child.

> The mother or nurse does not employ a jingle because it is a nursery rhyme *per se*, but because in the pleasantness (or desperation) of the moment it is the first thing which comes to mind.
>
> (Opie and Opie 1951: 6)

But more is happening here than the amusement of children or the learning of a set of words. In the interaction of the game, in the rocking of the lullaby, a loving relationship of trust and joint experience is being built up and cemented. When, in the classroom, I first read the following poem by Christina Rossetti to the children, they were enchanted:

Love me, I love you,
  Love me, my baby;
Sing it high, sing it low,
  Sing it as it may be.

Mother's arms under you,
  Her eyes above you
Sing it high, sing it low,
  Love me, I love you.

They responded, I think, not only to the gentle lyricism of the verse, or the seemingly effortless rocking of the rhythm, but to the unexpressed memories it engendered of comfort and trust, of their own babyhood in the security of their mothers' arms.

Nursery rhymes are so very important for small children, I suggest, because they become personal and because the children use them to build and to define relationships. When Lauren announced, 'Me and my mum sing that,' she was claiming the rhyme as family property. It was not her rhyme, but theirs, part of who she and her mother were and what they did together. Similarly, the children who proudly said they had sung a particular rhyme at playgroup made sure I knew which playgroup they meant and which children had attended it. It was part of a shared experience that forged them together as a group. They wanted me to know who was and who was not included. Even Kitty and Daisy, with their insistence on 'That's my one!', were using the rhymes to define themselves as individuals. 'This rhyme is the property of Kitty and not Daisy. We are not the same, and I am a separate person' seemed to be the message.

The rhymes, then, have a positive effect: they affirm children in their relationships and they establish their individuality. This goes some way, perhaps, towards explaining how children use nursery rhymes. It says nothing about why they are attractive in the first place or what is their lasting appeal.

Nursery rhymes are strong. The origins of many are obscure and some rhymes are ancient. The Opies (1951) discovered that at least 25 per cent of those we know today were probably current in Shakespeare's time. They are predominantly oral traditions. As a child, I never owned a nursery-rhyme book; nor do most of the children in my class. Yet, between us, we know a vast number of rhymes. The rhymes survive, passed on from adult to child, changing as language and circumstance require.

Oral rhymes are the true waifs of our literature in that their original wording, as well as their authors, are usually unknown. But this does not mean that they are necessarily sickly strays to whom only the indulgent and undiscriminating nursery will give shelter. Rather it is true that having to fend for themselves, without the benefit of sponsor or sheep-skin binding, they have had to be wonderfully fit to have survived.

(Opie and Opie 1963: 7)

They are fit. They are lithe and energetic, and ready to play. They have immediacy:

Jack be nimble,
Jack be quick,
Jack jump
Over the candlestick.

They are technically faultless. Either the years and usage have pruned away imperfection or, more likely, their virtuosity in the first place has made them memorable. They all have a strong and regular pulse, yet within that pulse metres can vary and frolic as much as the form and subject matter will allow. Here is an example:

Hickory dickory dock
The mouse ran up the clock.
The clock struck one
The mouse ran down.
Hickory dickory dock.

No child stops to notice how the mouse scurries up the clock with scampering dactyllic feet, or how the slower iambic metre of the middle lines echoes the chiming of the hour. The Jack rhyme is just as effective. He is made physically to jump over that candlestick by rhythm alone. It is impossible to say line three, with those two strongly stressed syllables at the beginning followed by three unstressed ones, without a leap and a running landing. This virtuoso marriage of form and content is not unusual in nursery rhymes, and must be part of their strength and appeal.

So, too, must be the games that so many of them play with sound and language. 'Hey diddle diddle, the cat and the fiddle' is simply fun to say. It reproduces (or perhaps initiates) the sort of word game that young children find so attractive. The verses glitter with rhyme and alliteration.

But though the technical brilliance of nursery rhymes undoubtedly makes them easier to remember, their lasting strength cannot reside in that alone. There must be something more in their matter to make them so sustaining to small children. John Goldthwaite (1996) explores this issue. He makes two main points. One is that nursery rhymes are useful. They provide the child with a vast cast-list of eccentrics, all eager to be recognised and befriended, as well as a catalogue of lore about numbers, the weather and animals that helps the child to comment on and negotiate a path through everyday life.

His second point is that nursery rhymes are make-believe and part of nonsense. This he defines as 'a flirtation with disorder, a turning upside down of the world for the pleasure of seeing it come right again'. This nonsense, which he calls *allsense*, is harmony: 'that which transports our sensible, disparate understandings into something – a kind of light perhaps – that precludes and justifies them all' (1996: 16).

For Goldthwaite, allsense is a quality that can be found in all really good children's literature. It is not something that can be deliberately written in and cannot be found for the looking. It is 'the enlightening ether that touches the child with a quickening gladness' (p. 16). It is, if I might borrow from Goldthwaite's theological vocabulary, grace – a sense of joyous liberty and rightness that comes free with the work.

Well, perhaps it is this that children recognise and cherish in nursery rhymes. Certainly there is a grace and a lightness of touch in the best of them, and a joy, a spirited eagerness for life, that many children appreciate. When they come to school, aged nearly 5, they carry it with them – a great, positive treasure hoard of knowledge of and enthusiasm for verse. What happens to it when they come through the playground gates will be considered next.

In the playground

One morning in the playground where I was on duty a pair of year 2 girls sang:

> I saw a box of matches
> Upon the kitchen floor, floor, floor,
> And when I wasn't looking
> They danced upon the floor, floor, floor.
> Singing aye, aye, yippee, yippee aye.
> Singing aye, aye, yippee, yippee aye.
> Singing aye, aye yippee
> Granny's such a hippie
> Aye, aye yippee, yippee aye.

With the song went a complicated clapping ritual. To begin, they stood facing each other. On the first and all subsequent unstressed syllables of the verse, they clapped. On each stress, they put their hands in front of them, palms forward, and clapped each other's hands. For the chorus, the girls put their own hands together and swung their arms across their bodies, brushing the backs of each other's hands in time with the beat. It looked good fun.

Games such as this are common in the playground. Clusters of girls, usually around 7 years of age, are the main participants. Sometimes they graciously and somewhat patronisingly initiate a younger child. Occasionally that child is a boy. (I have watched little boys, from reception and year 1 classes, look on wistfully at these performances, longing for a turn, but rightly suspecting that it was not to be – at least, not in public!)

These rhymes are lively and energetic – and meaningless. The fun of them is in the movement, the physical mastery of clapping and singing and of keeping the rhythm going all at the same time. As with nursery rhymes, rhythm is important: it is part of the structure that makes them memorable. And even more than nursery rhymes, this form stems from an oral tradition. The rhymes are passed on from child to child, from generation to generation, and it is this that makes them distinctive.

> While the nursery rhyme passes from the mother or another adult to the small child on her knee, the school rhyme circulates simply from child to child, usually outside the home and beyond the influence of the family circle. By its nature a nursery rhyme is a jingle preserved and propagated not by children but by adults, and in this sense it is an 'adult' rhyme. It is a rhyme that is adult approved. The schoolchild's verses are not intended for adult ears. In fact part of the fun is the thought, usually correct, that adults know nothing about them.
>
> (Opie and Opie 1959: 1)

In this way the playground rhyme is the prodigal son of the nursery rhyme, and John Goldthwaite would therefore probably not approve of it. Nowhere is the benevolent wisdom of Mother Goose, or even of a real mother, guiding her charges and readers along the paths of right thinking, better illustrated. Iona Opie (1993) lurks benignly with her notebook in a playground in Hampshire, but she is a spectator. She offers no advice and makes no judgements. These rhymes have left home with half the family fortune and no blessing. They thrive beyond adult approval. They are independent and determinedly proud to be so.

But the family resemblance is strong. The gentle finger play of 'pat-a-cake' has become the vigorous clapping game, with arms flailing, hands slapping and skirts lifting. Children jump, turn, stretch, bump, touch the ground and do all the other actions that accompany the rhymes, and part of the fun is to do them as fast and as furiously as possible. The occasional rhyme is still there: but nowadays the need to comment on the weather has abated. Something more pertinent is required:

Liar, liar
Your pants
are on fire!

the children in my class chant with relish.

There is a need, too, now that there is no adult to arbitrate, to find a fair way to settle disputes. Dipping games are a useful way to sort out turn taking:

> Ibble obble black bobble
> Ibble obble out.
> If you see a policeman
> Punch him on the snout.
> What colour was his blood?

In every way these rhymes are rougher and readier than those of the nursery. They have no time for the fastidious. Part of their appeal to children is that they celebrate all the rude words of which adults disapprove. Thus, underwear, nakedness, bodily functions, blood, gore and sex are all named as often as possible. The rhymes do this not to annoy adults, for adults know little about them; rather they indicate that they and the children who say them are not part of adult culture and that adult strictures have no place in their world.

Just as nursery rhymes define who you are in the home, so playground rhymes draw the distinctions in the playground. The intimacy of friendship finds expression in the clapping game. Taunts and insults separate enemies. A rude verse might impress upon friends the bravado of the speaker, and the shared giggling about it afterwards is expressive of companionship. Songs and rhymes are worn like badges in the playground to mark belonging or the desire to belong.

> I never felt more
>   like singing the blues
> When Ipswich win
>   and Norwich lose.
> Oh Ipswich—
>   Got me singing the blues.

sing the little boys in my class. 'My brother told me that,' said Ben, 'and we sing it. Us.' And he put his arms round the shoulders of his two best friends. As he did so, he staked a claim not only for the companionship of Adam and Mark but for membership of a wider social group – the big boys who like football, and even the supporters on the terraces.

Girls too use lyrics in this way. The Spice Girls are very popular in my classroom at the moment. The girls wear Spice Girls-emblazoned T-shirts for PE. They bring in photographs and magazines about the group; in the playground, they 'become' one Spice Girl or another – they each have a favourite. They adopt an entirely uncharacteristic (for them) demeanour, a whiny voice and then sing the songs and dance the routine. It's the sort of playground game I would expect to see from 10-year-olds. The children in my class are 5. Their favourite is the hit-song *Wannabe*, and much of the attraction seems to be in the lyrics. There the invitation to tell what you want, what you really want, is repeated, embroidered, manipulated in a way that reminds me more than anything else of the monologues small children sometimes deliver as they fall asleep. The word-play is there, as is the rhythmic repetition of sounds. There is a circular quality about it. Words and rhythms come again and again for the sake of sound alone. No wonder small children like this: they recognise it. The Spice Girls have hit on a formula that enables these little children to affirm their own creativity with language and, at the same time, to express their kinship with and desire to be accepted by much older girls.

But initiation into the culture where playground rhymes and popular songs thrive is gradual. The children do not come to school and find themselves immediately embroiled in it. There seems to be a time, lasting for about a year, when the children belong neither entirely to the comfortable culture of the home, where they are nourished by nursery rhymes, nor to the wilder world of the playground into which they have yet to be accepted. What happens then to the poetry in their heads is likely to depend on the classroom.

In the classroom

The poetry the children and I enjoyed together in the classroom was plentiful and varied. It came from different traditions and a number of sources. We read poets who were established nursery favourites, such as Rossetti, Milne and Stevenson; we read modern black poets, particularly Bloom and Nichols. We read 'funny' poems written specially for children (Rosen, Prelutsky and Foster) and serious poems written for adults (Auden, Frost).

The poems we read were nearly always selected by me, and I chose only those that gave me pleasure. I was never constrained by the usefulness of a poem's subject matter. If it complemented the work we were doing elsewhere in the curriculum, then that was a bonus, not a requirement. I chose poems with an eye and an ear to what the children would like and what I thought would interest them.

Typically, what happened when we read poems was that the children would all come and sit on the carpet and be ready to listen while I read. I would introduce the poem and the poet, and would give any clues I thought necessary to focus the children on what was to come ('You have to imagine the poet is. . . . See if you can hear the bit about . . .'). Sometimes I merely said: 'See if you like this.' Then I would read the poem and ask: 'What do you remember? What did you like?'

There would be a flurry of hands in the air, and I would do my best to give everyone a chance to speak. Many children would repeat to me the final phrase of the poem, and some only the last word. Others, usually the more mature children, would remember a line or a phrase or an image from the poem. It interested me that they always tried to give me the exact words they had heard, although I never insisted they should. I was always ready to help out if their attempts faltered, and this pleased them. They seemed to know instinctively that the crafting of the words mattered. We would talk over what they had remembered and rejoice and wonder at the coincidences. Then I would read the poem again.

What happened next would depend on the poem itself. Sometimes we would continue to do little more than notice and remember. Sometimes we would pursue an idea or a wondering voiced by one of the children. At other times I would direct them to listen for particular features or ask them what the poem made them think. Sometimes it was more appropriate to play, and that's what we would do, experimenting with tempo and voices for the fun of performing it. Whatever we did, I always tried to end the session with another reading of the poem, so that the experience of the text itself would remain in the children's minds. By now, of course, many of them were ready to join in, and frequently they did.

Poems with insistent rhythms and strong rhymes were always popular. One favourite was Foster's *Marty Smarty*:

> Marty Smarty went to a party
> In her jumbo jet
> After tea she jumped in the sea
> And got her pants all wet.

The children learned them by heart almost instantly and enjoyed the fun and the achievement of knowing the words. Such poems have features in common with the rhymes of the playground: Foster mentions underwear and uses a four line verse form that is typical of popular children's rhymes. Indeed his poem shares form and rhymes with a much ruder example with a similar theme recorded in the playground by Iona Opie (1993: 31). Doubtless this accounts for some of its appeal, marking it out as an object of play, which the pounding rhythms accentuate and confirm.

Grace Nichols' *Ar-A-Rat* is rather different:

> I know a rat on Ararat
> He isn't thin, he isn't fat . . .

It, too, pounds with rhyme and rhythm, the beat stressing the frequently repeated *at*-rhymes. At first the children loved it for the rhythm and the predictability of the rhyme, but then things seemed to change. 'My favourite bit,' said Lauren one day, 'is where it says: "Eyes like saucers glow in the dark".' Flora began to speculate on the ending. 'I think he's the last to leave Noah's Ark because he wants to think about things; ponder why the world is green, and that', she said. It seemed to me that the interest in this poem for them had begun to move away from an almost physical inter-action with the structure and to change into a more intimate exploration of its subject. The girls appeared to be picking up something of the change in tone and pace at the end of the poem. They were noticing imagery and making of it an invitation to wonder. This they seemed to find satisfying.

Mark, trying to sum up his continuing delight in this poem, many weeks after we had last aired it in the classroom, told me: ' Well, I like it because it tells you all about the rat. He isn't thin, he isn't fat. He's just medium-sized really. That's what I like about it.' I think what he was trying to express was that here was a poem that was worth taking into your head and spending time thinking about. Pounding rhythms helped initially: they are attractive, and enable one to remember the poem easily, but the best poems have more substance.

I realised early on that teaching Isobel was going to be rewarding. It was a dark, snowy afternoon and we were all weary. I decided to read Robert Frost's *Stopping by Woods on a Snowy Evening*. This seems to me to be an extraordinarily effective poem: the rhythm, gentle and persistent; the lines, rarely end-stopped, drawing the reader on to follow the line of thought through to the end of each idea; the rhyme, long vowel sounds, repeated, bridging the stanzas; the sigh of the alliteration: all this turning the poem in on itself, making it as hypnotic as watching snow. The effect is reflec-tive, ponderous, mesmerising. The children loved it.

I was hardly aware of Isobel as I read it to the class that first time. Hers was not one of the hands that waved at me, of children desperate to say what they remembered. She sat quietly and waited till everyone had finished. Then, very calmly and seriously, she said: 'I really like that poem. Say it again.'

I did, and this time I watched her. I saw how she sat, all concentration, back straight, head inclined towards me, smiling appreciatively. She was listening to the sound the poem made, and finding it good. It seemed to be an almost musical appreciation. She was responding to the cadence, the rise and fall of my voice as I read it, the regularity of metre, the tune of the piece. She was finding aesthetic pleasure in it.

I continued to be astonished by Isobel. One day she told me that a lullaby we sometimes read was 'a really beautiful poem'. It seemed a strange expres-sion for a 5-year-old, and I wondered if it was the sort of judgement she had been encouraged to make at home. It appeared not. When I spoke to her mother, she was most surprised. There were no books of poems in the house and no one gave poetry a thought. Even nursery rhymes had stopped long ago. Then a memory: Isobel as a baby had sat upon her grandfather's knee while he had recited Gaelic verse to her. The child understood not one word of what he said, but had listened to the cadence, the rhythm, the alliteration, and had loved every minute. 'She always', said her mother, 'wanted more.'

Isobel refined her listening skills as the year went on. By the end of the summer term she was able to use them analytically. She could say that she liked poems to be 'singy'. *Marty Smarty* was 'fast' and 'just silly'; Christina Rossetti was more to her taste. *Hurt No Living Thing* was a favourite.

> Hurt no living thing:
>   Ladybird nor butterfly,
> Nor moth with dusty wing,
>   Nor cricket chirping cheerily,
> Nor grasshopper so light of leap,
>   Nor dancing gnat, nor beetle fat,
> Nor harmless worms that creep.

It was not 'fast' like a playground rhyme, not 'slow' like a lullaby: it was 'fast *and* slow'. With only a little help she managed to express that she could hear a change of pace in the poem: the slow, steady, emphatic stresses of the first line, and the faster, lighter metre of 'cricket chirping cheerily'. I was not surprised that Isobel could hear these differences. What impressed me was that she could tell it. To do so presupposes an awareness of rhythm that can only have been achieved by reflection and analysis.

The poems we read together came alive for the children in my class and danced in their imaginations. One day, Isobel told me this about stories: 'When I go home they stay in my head, and I go upstairs to play and I have my tea and they are *still there*!' It was the same with poems. Flora twice told me how she would 'tell' the poems we knew to her mother, 'and my mum said, "What a lovely poem!"' Occasionally, the children would bring me scraps of paper from home, with snippets of familiar verse written on them. In the classroom, Hannah bubbled over with verse. 'And miles to go before I sleep', she announced out of the blue one Friday afternoon. Everybody within hearing chorused the last line.

Another time, in the excitement before swimming, Hannah could hardly contain her glee:

> 'Give yourself a hug
> when you feel unloved'

she chanted. Nichols' poem expressed her contentedness with life. It was a sunny summer afternoon, she was going swimming with her friends, and her mother and sister were there, too. School was wonderful. She was wonderful. Life was one enormous affirmative hug. The poem exactly complemented her mood. Hannah was the girl who as a very small child had referred to nursery rhymes whenever she could. Here was a development: whereas, before, a word or a concrete experience of something like rain would have suggested a rhyme, now she was able to reflect on herself and find words from a poem that chimed with her feelings.

Louise Rosenblatt (1978) describes how she investigated the process by which adult readers come to understand poems. She tells how she encouraged people to record their impressions and to note how their ideas changed and developed as they read. What she discovered was that the reading of poetry is a personal and complicated process. Typically, readers' first impressions were personal: they found in the texts echoes of their own preferences, ideas and experiences. They made provisional hypotheses based on these interests, and the hypotheses changed as they read. There was a continual revisiting and revising of ideas. First impressions were considered, and upheld or rejected in light of other, less immediate, parts of the text. Readers moved in and out of the poem, walking around it as if it were a sculpture, considering it from different angles, until eventually they came to some sort of satisfactory understanding.

It seems that the children in my class were doing much the same with the poems they heard. They took home in their heads the bits they liked. They played with them, considered them, tried them out. When we read the poem again, they thought some more. Eventually, ideas were assimilated and judgements made. When Mark said that he liked *Ar-A-Rat* because the rat was medium-sized, he was still engaging in this process. When Flora wondered why the rat was the last to leave the ark, so was she. And Hannah, when she blurted out 'Give yourself a hug', was doing much the same thing. She was discovering what the poem meant to her and affirming what it was good for.

Flora said one day: 'When I watch a video, or read a story or listen to a poem, I think about it and think about it and think about it, and then I get to understand it more. The more I think about it, the more I understand.' Here, I suggest, is the difference between the way in which the children dealt with the rhymes they knew from home and the poetry we read in the classroom. The process of understanding was different. In the classroom, the children were invited to look inwards, inside themselves, inside the poems. It is difficult to do that with nursery rhymes; they are too transparent. Whereas nursery rhymes were understood in relation to other people, the poems were reflected upon by each child individually and understood in relation to herself or himself. Thus Isobel could pursue her interest in the tune of the poetry. Flora could muse over meanings and Hannah could take into her head as much as she could remember, and use it and display it exactly as she pleased.

Conclusions

> Only one in a million-billion-thrillion-zillion
> like me

By the end of the summer term, the oldest children in my class had passed their sixth birthday and the youngest were just weeks away from their fifth. All of them knew a lot about poetry and none of them was afraid of it.

From their homes and their playgroups they had brought with them to school a wealth of knowledge about song and nursery rhyme, and now, in the playground, they were beginning to learn the rhymes and the songs and the word games that were current there. A seamless transition was taking place. As the need for the homely comforts and the stories of nursery rhymes waned, the more boisterous and anarchic surprises of the playground waited in the wings. As the children grew away from the physical memories of nursery play that had helped define their relationships within the home, so a new batch of games and rhymes presented itself to help them negotiate their way in the wider society of the playground. Something similar but different was happening with the poetry in the classroom. There was still rhyme and rhythm, and the fun of sharing them with friends. There was chanting and whispering, performing and giggling. There was something more, too. There was wondering and there was reflection. There was an invitation not just to wonder if you had ever fallen down a hill and bumped your head but whether you really could see stars reflected in a bucket and how wonderful it would be if they danced in your imagination after the grownups had chased you in. There was the chance to hear poems and think 'Yes. I really believe that' or 'I know how that feels'. There was the opportunity to sit back with Isobel and simply say 'I like the sound of that.'

I like the sound. Here is the change in emphasis. Not 'we like it', 'me and my mum', or 'me and my new friend', but 'I'. The focus has turned inwards. It is not the relationship with other people that is explored as children come to terms with these texts; it is, I suggest, the relationship with themselves and with poetry. This seems to me to be important. For it is in the exploration of these relationships that children find the resources with which to affirm the people they are and the choices they make.

'All poetry is magic' says Charles Causley (1974). Louise Rosenblatt, I think, would agree. She writes about the transformation that has to take place in the reader's understanding if the text on the page is to become a living poem in the reader's head. That sounds like magic to me. Yet it is a magic I saw performed in the classroom again and again as the children took over the poems we read together and created them afresh for themselves.

What will happen to these children? Will the magic continue? Will they continue to find poems to love and enjoy, to think about and play with? Will poetry continue to affirm them as individuals?

Two happenings at the end of term give me hope. Mark came to school with two sheets of A4 paper folded together. 'Look!' he said. 'I've made a poem book.' On the front was written 'Mark's Poem Book'. Inside was an adaptation of a couplet from Rossetti's *What Is Pink?*, a line or two from *Hurt No Living Thing*, and his own sea poem. 'I'm going to make a poem book too', said all his friends. And they did.

Isobel came to school looking immensely pleased with herself. 'My mum's going to buy me a poem book.' A day or two later it arrived, crisply new, in the classroom. It was Milne's *Now We Are Six*. Together we read it. Together we performed *The Good Little Girl* to the rest of the class. And Isobel, whose reading is not yet fluent, swelled in importance and confidence as we did so.

May this be the first of many collections and anthologies that she owns. May they nourish her. May her confidence continue to grow and may it always be affirmed by the poetry she loves.

Afterword

Somebody – John Stannard, I think – said that what teachers were likely to find new and difficult about the Literacy Hour was the requirement to work with children on texts at 'word level'. I'm not sure that he is right. For it seems to me that faced with a class of 5-year-olds and a nursery rhyme, say, *Hickory Dickory Dock*, the easiest thing in the world is to 'do' phonemic and syllabic awareness. It is natural behaviour for a reception teacher to clap out the rhythm (which amounts to the same thing as recognising the syllables) and to play with the rhymes, perhaps substituting *sock*, *frock*, *rock* and *pock* for *dock* and *clock*. Hilarity always ensues: this is the stuff of early years' classrooms.

Far more difficult, I think, is working at text level. *The National Literacy Strategy* (DfEE 1998) unhelpfully defines this as 'comprehension'. If it means expecting children to answer questions such as 'Who ran up the clock?', then I am disappointed: for such banal and unchallenging questions are an insult to everyone. Inferential questions – perhaps: 'What do you think made the mouse run down?' Or suppositional ones: 'Why do you suppose it ran up the clock in the first place?' – are no better: they miss the point of the rhyme. If 'text level' is to mean anything in the context of poetry, then I want it to be about exploring that point, about responding to the text in its entirety, and experiencing what Causley calls magic.

The magic of *Hickory Dickory Dock* is in its fun: understanding it as a whole text needs to acknowledge this. And if its fun resides, as I have suggested, in the nonsense and mechanics of the verse, then it is best taught by encouraging the children to appreciate those elements. So let them enjoy the rhymes and the rhythms, and if work at text level is indistinguishable from work at word level, then so be it. That is the nature of nursery rhyme – and of early years.

Other texts are less transparent and can support an exploration of meaning. We first read Frost's *Stopping By Woods On a Snowy Evening* very quietly. We listened to the poem for the sounds and silences within it. The children heard the bells for themselves and were enchanted by 'the sweep of easy wind and downy flake'. The mood of the poem was established. We read it again, and again, and allowed the tune and the tone and the words to seep into our minds and affect us. Gently, thoughtfully, we reflected on the words, wondered about the man, his promises and the attraction of the snowy woods. We allowed the poem to speak. This is understanding at text level. It is not easy to achieve. What the teacher needs is time, patience, the confidence to carry it off and a passionate belief in the worth of the poem and of children as makers of meaning.

Working at word level is much easier. It is not difficult to imagine a whole class lesson on 'ee' from this poem. I hope it is never done. To do it would be destructive: the poem fragmented, and its magic reduced to clay. The challenge is in finding tasks that work *with* poems rather than against them. I might, for example, give children a copy of a poem with the rhymes missing and those words on cards. As they reassemble the text, they practise grapho-phonic recognition and use semantic and syntactic cues in the best Literacy Hour fashion. But the poem is built up, the text is not broken into a disembodied exercise, and the children's experience of it continues. As with *Hickory Dickory Dock*, this work at word level complements the text. It helps build an understanding of how the poem is made.

Reading poetry is an affective experience. If we value poetry, and children's responses to it, then we will use it as part of the Literacy Hour. But we must handle it with care, guard its integrity and not let its power and magic be diminished.

References

The Literature

Causley, C. (1974) *The Puffin Book of Magic Verse*, London: Puffin.

DfEE (1998) *The National Literacy Strategy*, London: DfEE.

Goldthwaite, J. (1996) *The Natural History of Make-Believe*, New York and Oxford: Oxford University Press.

Meek, M. (1991) *On Being Literate*, London: Bodley Head.

Opie, I. (1993) *The People in the Playground*, Oxford: Oxford University Press.

Opie, I. and Opie, P. (1951) *The Oxford Dictionary of Nursery Rhymes*, Oxford: Oxford University Press.

—— (1959) *The Lore and Language of School Children*, Oxford: Oxford University Press.

—— (1963) *The Puffin Book of Nursery Rhymes*, London: Puffin.

Rosenblatt, L. (1978) *The Reader, the Text, the Poem*, South Illinois University Press.

Poems mentioned or quoted in the text

John Foster: *Marty Smarty*, in J. Foster (ed.) (1996) *Chanting Rhymes*, Oxford: Oxford University Press.

Robert Frost: *Stopping By Woods on a Snowy Evening*, in K. Webb (ed.) (1979) *I Like This Poem*, London: Puffin.

A. A. Milne: *The Good Little Girl* in A. A. Milne (1927) *Now We are Six*, London: Methuen.

Grace Nichols: *Give Yourself a Hug*, in G. Nichols (1996) *Give Yourself a Hug*, London: Puffin. *Ar-A-Rat*, in J. Agard, and G. Nichols (1996) *A Caribbean Dozen*, London: Walker Books.

Christina Rossetti: *Love Me – I Love You*; *Hurt No Living Thing*; and *What Is Pink?*, in C. Rossetti (1968 [1872]) *Sing-Song*, New York: Dover Publications, Inc.

R. L. Stevenson: *Escape At Bedtime*, in R. L. Stevenson (1926) *A Child's Garden of Verses*, London: Bodley Head.

Chapter 2

'Never be without a *Beano*!'

Comics, children and literacy

Helen Bromley

beano . . . *n.*, *pl.* **beanos**. *Brit. slang.* A celebration, party or other enjoyable time.

(Collins Concise Dictionary)

As a child, everything about being a *Beano* reader seemed magical. The satisfying sound as the newspapers dropped on the mat, the anticipation as you found the precious comic in the folds of a newspaper, the blessed regularity with which it appeared, no matter what, and the wonderful way that your surname was written across the top by the newsagent, emphasising the fact that this was your comic and no one else's. After all this, came the magic of reading the comic itself. For me the approach was ritualistic. Find somewhere relatively private, curl up and work through the comic in the order that I deemed to be appropriate. A very conformist child, I would always read the front cover first, even though Biffo the Bear was not my favourite character, then to the middle to see what the Bash St. Kids were up to, and then in order of preference until the whole comic had been read. One reading was never enough. There were jokes to be savoured over and over again, and sometimes puzzling references that needed to be mulled over, until they were understood to my own satisfaction.

Part of the pleasure that I gained from being a reader of comics was the secure anticipation that favourite characters would be as they always were, the reassurance that they would not let you down and that, although each adventure was new, the individual stories carried with them certain expectations, created by your understanding of specific personalities and their idiosyncratic ways. In having this knowledge, readers are made to feel experts, having their predictions confirmed on a regular basis. There was no doubt about it, reading the *Beano* made you feel clever. Not only that, but along with other *Beano* readers you were part of a club, 'in the know', specialists in a particular field.

Twice a year, you had the opportunity to enjoy your favourite *Beano* characters in other formats. The first was the *Beano Summer Special*, a sort of bumper edition of the comic which included special features, and, if you were lucky, more than one story about your favourite characters from the weekly edition. There was also a tendency for the *Summer Special* to offer a variety of story-telling formats: double-page spreads involving, for example, the Bash St. Kids at the beach, would require a different type of reading from the usual strip cartoon style of storytelling found in the comic itself. These pages would be telling a complete story when looked at overall, but the pleasure then came in seeking out the individual character-related jokes that the author and illustrator had scattered throughout. Better even than the *Summer Specials* were the *Beano Annuals*, an essential part of my Christmas for many years. Always left at the foot of the bed on Christmas Eve, they were one of the first things that I looked for on waking. Themed for the winter season, these annuals provided hours of pleasure with the same mix of characters as the weekly edition, but in greater abundance. Often the front and back covers told stories in their own right, such as when Biffo the Bear was shown on the front cover of the annual dressed as a strongman, apparently lifting extremely heavy weights. Regular readers of the comic were also likely to notice the birds with very sharp beaks hovering around either end of the dumb-bell. Sure enough, when you turned to the back cover, the birds had burst Biffo's weights, confirming the reader's predictions and completing the joke. It was also in the annuals that characters tended to spill over into each other's stories – something that was very rare in the weekly editions. In the annuals, Billy the Whizz, Dennis the Menace, Minnie the Minx and the rest were not just drawings in a comic but residents of Beanotown who related both to the regular characters within their individual strips and to each other. The intertextuality gave the stories another layer for the reader to savour – the cross-referencing meaning far more if you were a regular *Beano* reader.

The creators of the *Beano* were also extremely skilled at using texts other than the comic, in order to entertain and fascinate their readers. References were made to texts which might have been considered outside the normal reading boundary for those who read the *Beano*. In a Christmas *Beano Annual* from the mid-1960s a double-page spread showed the Bash St. Kids' futile attempt to learn poetry. Their teacher was using the works of Robert Burns, and the author of this particular story had played about with such famous lines as 'wee sleekit, cowerin timorous beastie' and 'My love is like a red, red rose, that newly blooms in June'. These had been parodied by Smiffy, Plug and other members of the gang, causing their teacher enormous irritation. This was my first introduction to the poetry of Robert Burns, and the original lines have stayed with me, far longer than the parodied version! In another annual, while Walter and his chums are singing a song, the reader is instructed by means of an aside: 'Sing to the tune of "Nymphs and Shepherds".'

These examples illustrate how the creators of the *Beano* viewed its readership when they were shaping the comic. The reader was never underestimated, always regarded as an active thinker, a problem solver, willing to make sense of what he or she was reading. Implicit in such references as the Burns example is the assumption that the reader will want to discover who Robert Burns was, and would find the tune to *Nymphs and Shepherds* somehow. (In my case, my mother supplied the answer to the first, and I was still able to sing the first line of the second when asked to do so by my own daughter!) Implicit in all this is the reader's willingness to be part of the joke, and use information gained from previous issues to create new understandings.

Comics in the home

As a child I was not encouraged to read the *Beano* because I would thereby acquire knowledge of classic poetry! My parents valued comics for their own sake – because they were funny, and also because they remembered enjoying comics themselves. So comics were seen as part of a broad reading diet, one which afforded opportunities for shared jokes and discussion about the characters and their adventures. Although many of the characters change with the generations – Big Eggo who adorned the very first *Beano* cover and Biffo the Bear, a cover star from the 1960s, no longer feature – certain characters, like Dennis the Menace, endure over time. These characters in particular provide a reservoir of shared knowledge that can be used for comparison and reflection.

The inter-generational possibilities of comics are fascinating; they seem to be part of the literary heritage that exists within some families. Enjoyed and valued by one generation, the next is encouraged to engage with similar texts, in the hope that such pleasures will be replicated. Of course, the sharing of common texts also offers opportunities to explain the literary heritage of the family to any new members, and to establish a context for those children's own literacy development. There is no guarantee that the younger generation will be willing to take on all aspects of their literacy inheritance. Times and contexts change; each reader has tastes and preferences which cannot be denied. My daughter, for example, although as enthusiastic about the *Beano* as I had been, merely tolerated Rupert Bear whom I had always thought quite magical. The rhyming couplets, which I had found so cleverly constructed, she thought were twee. However, the texts that *are* found to be acceptable will be forming an important part of the definition of what it means to be a reader in that particular home.

With all this in mind my daughter was encouraged to have the *Beano* from a very early age, in fact as soon as she could decode it for herself. She had been read to from a wide range of texts since she was very young, but, as Margaret Meek says: 'It is well nigh impossible to read [a comic] to a child. To read one with a child an adult has to be accepted as a peer, and even this is thought of as a kind of intrusion.'[1] With comics such as the *Beano* the role of the adult is to provide and to participate in discussions which have been initiated by the child itself. To try to be more is to try to break into a secret society while a meeting is in progress.

Watching my daughter with the *Beano* has been a fascinating experience. It has been obvious that, as she has got older, she has been able to understand more of its layers of meaning, but the sense of enjoyment and the development of loyalty to the characters have been there right from the very beginning. Like Michael Rosen in *Talking Pictures*,[2] who analysed his son's *Beano* reading, I interviewed my daughter Rebecca (then aged 8) and asked her what made the *Beano* so important to her. I think her answers demonstrate quite clearly the reading lessons that comics can teach children. At the time, we were looking at the front cover of the comic.

Question: What do the people who put the Beano together want you to do, as a reader, do you think?

Rebecca was quite explicit in her answer to this question:

'First of all, they want you to buy it. They want you to think it's really good. On the front it always says something like 'Never be without a *Beano*', or it has a free gift, or it tells you it's the UK's No. 1 comic. I expect that they're hoping that once you've bought it, you will buy it every week – it tells you on the front that it's every Thursday. That's so that you don't just buy it once and forget about it. It's so that you will try and get it again. Get your mum and dad to buy it for you or something like that.'

Rebecca was very conscious of the act of purchasing the comic, where special trips had to be made to the newsagents or supermarket in order to get her copy of the *Beano*.

Question: What do you think of the cover story? What do you especially like about it?

The characters on the cover are Dennis the Menace and his dog Gnasher. (The dog has particular appeal; he is a canine equivalent of his master – non-conformist, subversive and rascally!) The detail in Rebecca's answers showed how closely she read the comic every week.

'Well, I think it's good how they do the titles of the story. They really relate to the characters – so Dennis is written in black-and-red stripes, just like his jumper, Gnasher is written in furry writing because he's a dog. So even those titles give you an idea of the characters. The words aren't just plain. You know that this is Dennis and Gnasher's page. Also, Dennis and Gnasher always look at you, as if they are looking out of the comic world into your world. When they're doing this, they're inviting you in, they're saying, "Get involved with us, with our story".'

This way of explicitly acknowledging the reader is something that is a particular characteristic of a number of comics similar to the *Beano*. As Rebecca said: 'They expect you to understand. It's like they want to be in your company, as well as you in theirs.' This acknowledgement seems important. All of us want children to engage with the texts that they read at more than just a superficial level. In order to do this effectively, it is necessary for the reader to see something that is 'in it for them'. Children reading picture-books and novels will come across a wide range of authorial devices for involving them as readers, and those offered by the comic seem to be a way of familiarising readers with such devices.

Question: How did you learn to read the front page?

'It may look like an ordinary inside page – like a cartoon strip, in which case you know you have to go across the page like this [pointing with her finger]. There's more to it than that though. You also have to work out what happened in-between the pictures. Your brain has to work to fill in the gaps. The comics never tell you everything – there is always something for you to do. On other front covers, it may be one big picture – *these are difficult to read* [my italics], because you have to be sure that you don't miss anything. You might also get covers where it's not obvious which order you have to read the picture in.'

At this point I asked her what she did when faced with one of these pages.

'I take a guess at where it starts, then guess what's going to happen next, and look at the picture that I think fits. If it does, I do the same thing again, and so on. If it doesn't, well I go back to the beginning and have another try.'

What she has made explicit here is the sort of behaviour required of comic readers outlined by Margaret Meek, 'where the young reader becomes both the teller and the told, what Bakhtin calls "the dialogic imagination".[3] This type of thinking is required not just for the front cover, but throughout the comic.

Rebecca had already volunteered that she thought the *Beano* was 'very clever', so I asked her to explain what she meant by this. There were several aspects of the comic that seemed to contribute particularly to her judgement:

- The way the comic uses jokes, puns and alliteration: the names of the characters often rhyme (Dennis the Menace, Roger the Dodger), consist of puns (Les Pretend, a boy who changes into different people and/or things; Ball Boy who can turn into a ball; Ivy the Terrible; Joe King) or are alliterative (Minnie the Minx, Gnasher and Gnipper). In using these devices the authors of the comic show that they expect the reader to understand the joke, although the information required to interpret the joke may not be instantly accessible – how many average 8-year-olds would know of Ivan the Terrible?

- The variety of 'voices' in the comic: these include the sound effects, often words which seem genre-specific to comics, words like 'Cripes!', 'Yikes!', 'Bah!', 'Erk!', 'Glub!' These have to be read in conjunction with the rest of the story, and are often written in script which indicates how they are to be read. (Bold capitals, for example, or within specifically shaped speech bubbles.) As well as sound effects there is the voice of the narrator, conveyed by the text in the small boxes adjacent to the picture frames. With the minimum of text (But . . ., Then . . ., So . . ., etc.) they move the story on. Different to the voice of the narrator, but equally important, is the voice of the editor. This occurs in different forms. Often, the editor is used to control the characters' actions. In one episode of Pup Parade, the pups are shown lolling around the dustbin, with one saying: 'What'll we do today pups?' A second pup replies: 'Don't know. The *Beano* Editor hasn't sent us our story script to follow today.' The pups then proceed to write their own story for the artist to draw, finding that their greatest wish (a huge pile of bones) comes to life. The layers in this story alone would be fascinating enough for the reader, but all this is made more complex by the fact that pinned to the title of the episode is a roughly drawn comic script which reads

PICTURE 1	Pups laying around bin. Pug – 'What'll we do today pups?'
PICTURE 2	Tubby at open letter-box. 'Don't know! The *Beano* editor hasn't sent us our story script to follow today.'

So, although the pups thought they were in control of the plot, their lives were being manipulated, as always, by their author. The editor also controls by means of comments such as '"That's enough menacing" ED'. Readers of *Private Eye* will no doubt be familiar with this device. This type of storyline also empowers readers by allowing them into explicit knowledge of the production process of the comic. This reduces the inaccessibility of such texts, and encourages child readers to believe that they, too, could create comics. I shall return to this point.

- Intertextuality: the references to other texts and information has always been a significant feature of the *Beano* and, as with the words of Robert Burns quoted earlier, Rebecca feels that she has learned many items of what she describes as 'general knowledge-type things' from the comic (information, for example, about Mount Rushmore, the Spanish Armada, Latin verbs, James Bond, the Laughing Cavalier, *Mad Max 3*, $E=mc^2$ and Shakespeare – intertextuality in all its forms). Her favourite example is when Gnasher and Gnipper try to frighten off postmen of the world. This is where she learned about *lederhosen* – as the postmen from Austria were well protected from the 'gnashing and gnipping'.

These little snippets of information may seem to amount to nothing very much. They do, however, increase children's breadth of understanding of the adult world, but perhaps most importantly the authors of the *Beano* recognise that children want to be 'knowers of things', and that being in the know is empowering and can be used to influence those around you. I also believe that children remember the facts presented to them in a comic with greater facility than if they had read a physics text book or an atlas. They remember them because there is something incongruous about the type of information offered and the context within which it is presented. New pathways are then created for further learning, where additional information can be combined with existing knowledge and understanding increased. Rebecca remarked that the *Beano* teaches you things without you being aware of the learning, showing you things that teachers may have decided you were not yet old enough to know.

Like Michael Rosen's son, my daughter over several years became an expert *Beano* reader by compulsively scrutinising each issue. She also had to sit in a Buddha-like position, chin in hands, poring over it, until the last drop of pleasure had been gleaned from each weekly edition, then all the comics were kept safely and in order, a complete referencing system. She was (and still is) able to relate whole narratives from specific editions, and can explain jokes that she felt were especially clever.

Comics in the classroom

Following the discussions with my daughter, and having reflected on my own experiences, I decided to look at the status that was given to comics in my reception classroom. Until I had realised the potential of comics, they appeared mostly during wet dinnertimes, provided by the dinner ladies to keep the children amused and well behaved. There were no comics in my Book Corner, and I decided to rectify this situation by asking the children to bring some in from home. This was a mistake. Like my own daughter, the children in my class valued their comics and wanted to hang on to them at all costs. So, I bought a few to begin with and put them in a special box in the Book Corner. The effect was quite dramatic. Children who had not previously spent much time in the Book Corner began to do so, particularly boys. I provided a range of comics, including the *Beano*, media-related comics (more like magazines in style), *Playdays Magazine*, *Pingu*, *Postman Pat*, *Twinkle*. Once parents could see that comics are welcomed in the classroom, more examples appeared, especially those which made their intention to educate the reader quite explicit on the front cover, one even claiming to be 'Compatible with the National Curriculum'. Having noticed the increased use of the Book Corner after the introduction of comics, I wanted to see if the children in my reception class could analyse these texts in the same way that my daughter had done. I photocopied and enlarged the front page of one of the comics involved and we examined individually the title, price, illustrations and information about the contents. Then I asked the children a number of questions, including:

- Who do you think wrote these words?
- What do the people who wrote this want you to do after you have read what they have written?
- Why do you think the comic has a free gift?
- Who do you think is supposed to read the title, the contents, the price, etc?

The answers given by the children clearly showed their awareness of the different audiences that exist – parents, grandparents, newsagents and, of course, the children themselves. Perhaps the most interesting answer came when we were discussing the bar-code. I asked the children: 'Who reads the bar-code?' One child answered immediately: 'It's not a *who*, Mrs Bromley, it's a *what*. In fact it's several whats. It could be a beam of light at the checkout, a pen thing, or one of those things with a handle.' Of course, she was quite correct. It was also obvious that the children knew how they were being manipulated (or not) by the producers of comics. Free gifts and promises to teach children were identified as 'ways to get us to buy the comic'. One child pointed out: 'In the end, you only know if it's a good comic if you always get it. You can't always trust what it says on the front. They need to sell it to make money.' Quite complex understandings for children not yet 5 years of age.

I then interviewed the children about their comic-reading habits – who purchased them; how often they read them; were their comics important to them. The results were illuminating. On the whole, it was grandparents who tended to buy the comics, so they were regarded as a great treat, and often were part of the grandparents' regular visiting routine. Probably comics were not seen to be as valuable as books by the children's parents, but grandparents could indulge the children with them. One child was obviously a great *aficionado* of comics and knew an immense amount about them. (Incidentally, he was also a fan of cartoons, which tell stories in very similar ways.) When asked how he felt about them his reply was: 'I care for my comics.' Further investigation showed that he, like my daughter, kept them all in order, in a box in his bedroom. The introduction of comics to the classroom-texts that held interest for him showed him to be a positive reader: tenacious, perceptive and willing to spend sustained periods of time reading. It was then possible to introduce him to picture books in which comic-style illustrations and techniques are used: the books of Marcia Williams, for example. Every child comes to school with a different set of literacy practices, and these should be recognised in school. A colleague related how she had introduced *Teletubbies* comics to her reception class Book Corner with similar results. She said that children whom she had not perceived as readers now showed themselves to be so, thus raising her estimation of these children's capabilities.

Part of our weekly routine was a paired-reading session involving my reception class and a year 2 class. The year 2 class teacher agreed to hold a reading session using just comics. The results were fascinating. First, all the children were delighted to see the comics, and there was no reluctance on the part of any child to share a comic with his or her partner. Especially evident was that comics allow a variety of 'ways in' for the children. Although they were encouraged to share reading during normal sessions, the sharing in this session was of a particular intensity. It became apparent that within each comic there exist diverse text types, each one offering an opportunity for a regular reader of the title to be the expert. The children who were readers of the *Beano* obviously had their own favourite characters, and were sharing their in-depth knowledge of these characters, sometimes augmenting it with information gleaned from the Dennis the Menace cartoon shown on children's television. The *Beano* also has a fan club page on which readers' own contributions are highly valued; this page alone offers the opportunity to read jokes, photographs, adverts, addresses and application forms.

Comics such as *Thomas the Tank Engine* also provide more than simple narratives: they actually replicate many facets of magazines – puzzle pages, letter pages, 'facts about', articles, and photo-features offer within a single issue opportunities to each child to find a preferred reading style. When reading comics with others, these reading styles can be transferred from one child to another, thus broadening the reading repertoire.

What really struck me about how the children read comics was the way in which they used gesture to indicate their own fascination and also to draw in their reading partners. I took many photos at that particular session (none of them deliberately posed), and in each one child or another was pointing to some aspect of the comic. They were using their fingers to emphasise particular parts of the text under discussion, to demonstrate how to read certain types of page and also to influence and control. Although emergent readers often use their fingers when reading text, it is usually when they are unsure, or maybe, having 'dropped down a gear' in their reading, when they need support. But in this paired-reading session there was an air of confidence, of being in control, and of making decisions about the way the text should be read. (There is, of course, more choice in how you read a comic, than there is in how you read traditionally laid out narrative.) These signs and hand gestures seemed to make explicit and complex intellectual processes that were going on around the comics. Vygotsky[4] suggests that the acquisition of new concepts is mediated by signs. This was certainly evidenced in the children's behaviour with the comics. This knowledge is then internalised and used in the children's production of their own texts. Constructing a comic strip-style story is at least as intellectually challenging as reading one. In the process of production, children unpack the mystique that surrounds text, giving them ownership of the authorial devices used to entertain, inform and influence them. Looking at the story of Blob reproduced in Figure 2.1, created by a year 5 boy, shows just how much he had learned from his comics about devices for involving and entertaining the reader.

As with the characters in the *Beano*, Blob looks out at the readers, acknowledging them both in expression and through spoken greetings – 'Thank you, fans.' The hat and cane demonstrate that the child author is aware of the type of character who usually speaks such words – comedians from the music hall tradition. In the first frame, the scene is set, with the minimum of text, and the excitement of the character is evident in the lines used to indicate movement. As with any comic strip, we move rapidly to the next scenario, with the 'voice off' device telling us exactly where we are. The next three frames show a wide knowledge of the comic strip – the detailed drawings of the essential features, a minimal background which is nevertheless important (note the moralising role of the rabbit) and the use of sound effects – so typical of both comics and animated cartoons. The subsequent entry into the haystack and the collision with the lamp-post are true slapstick disaster, but they are accompanied by a secondary story line – that of the watching bird, first seen in the third frame. Close observers will note that the bird has collected a piece of the hay and is carrying it in its beak as the inevitable disaster is played out: an extremely clever marrying of the two story lines. As Blob is carried off with the traditional stars whirling around his head, no words are necessary to let the reader know that he is in safe hands, as one of the stretcher bearers is wearing an appropriate flag on his hat. The final scene brilliantly depicts a hospital, with the minimal amount of representation: a temperature chart, a leg in traction and a bedside table. Blob's feelings are indicated,

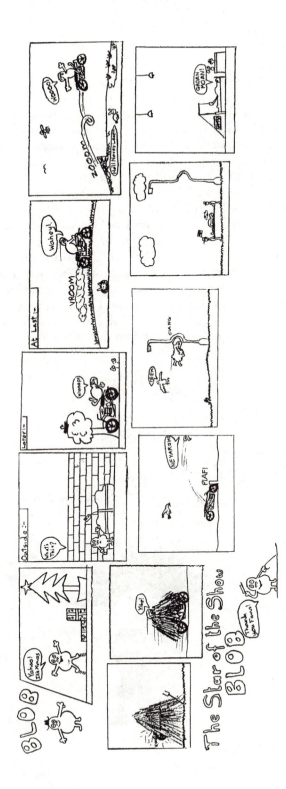

Figure 2.1 The story of Blob.

not in a long piece of direct speech but by a groan and a moan, which we know are loud because they have been written in capitals. It is a piece which powerfully demonstrates this child's mastery over one particular type of narrative. His reading of comics has powerfully influenced his ways of telling and enabled him to tell a story in a way which gives the reader challenges and entertainment of a sophisticated nature.

Young children also enjoy taking on the role of comic creator, as the pictures of Dennis the Menace and Sonic the Hedgehog, by Haroun Lazim aged 8, show (see Figures 2.2 and 2.3). The style of the original cartoon is imitated but also subverted. Readers familiar with Sonic the Hedgehog will recognise the influence on Dennis the Menace's hairstyle.

The combination of entertainment and intellectual challenge provided by comics is a powerful one. Victor Watson talks about children's fiction as 'the imaginative creation of a cultural space in which writers find ways of exploring what they want to say to and about children: an arena in which children and adults can engage in various kinds of shared and dynamic discourse'.[5] I would argue that this applies also to comics. In comics like the *Beano*, children are offered the widest choice of cultural spaces in which to

Figure 2.2 Dennis the Menace.

Figure 2.3 Sonic and Gnasher.

locate themselves. It is the visibility and the invisibility of these spaces which offer children such a broad range of experiences. Children may choose to locate themselves within the visible text and illustrations, but also to become a partner with the comic-book illustrator in the invisible – inhabiting narrative spaces time and time again.

Inevitably, comics like the *Beano* have had to change with the times – often creating public outcry in the process. Bash St. School was transformed into a glass-and-metal comprehensive to bring it up to date, but was returned to bricks and mortar after protests from readers. A change in Dennis the Menace's foot gear, from boots to trainers, received attention in the press and on the national news on TV. The *Beano* has just celebrated its sixtieth birthday, and although sales are not as high as they were, it is still tremendously popular. It has recognised the appeal of multimedia literacy to children, and you can now interact with your favourite characters by joining Dennis's Spider 'Dasher' (at www.beano.co.uk). Activities at the website include making the Bash St. Kids sing 'Happy Birthday' by 'clever use of the mouse' and being tested by Roger the Dodger to find out what your 'dodging level is'. It is this willingness to adapt that has no doubt helped the *Beano* to last so long.

I have no doubt of the significant part that comics have played in my own and my daughter's development as both readers and writers. Through reading the *Beano*, we have both developed a repertoire of jokes, understandings and ways of looking at the world that might not have been gained elsewhere. This comic has empowered Rebecca as reader in a number of ways. She has learned how to read 'writerly text', she understands a wide variety of uses of intertextuality, and she knows how cartoons can be used to persuade, inform and entertain. Perhaps most of all she has learnt some of the greatest pleasures that can come from sustained re-readings. In the same way that she savoured the *Beano*, and she now reads scripts of Victoria Wood sketches until she knows all the jokes, and is already (at 13) an avid reader of *Private Eye*.

As I have been writing this chapter, sitting in a study littered with copies of the *Beano*, Rebecca has come in to sit and read them yet again, searching in a determined fashion for old favourites. She commented that there are some stories which she understands more now than she did when she was younger, and on how she feels guilty that she does not have the *Beano* any more. (Her loyalties have been transferred to a range of pre-teenage magazines – *Smash Hits*, *Live and Kicking* and *Top of the Pops*.) This sense of guilt comes from the strong emotional attachment to everything the *Beano* represented – a vehicle through which children were empowered and treated as intelligent, knowing individuals. Comics command reader identification and involvement. To my mind, this alone would justify their place in the Book Corner of every classroom.

Notes

1   Meek, M. (1988) *How Texts Teach What Readers Learn*, Stroud: Thimble Press.
2   Rosen, M. (1996) 'Reading the *Beano*: a young boy's experience', in V. Watson and M. Styles (eds), *Talking Pictures*, London: Hodder & Stoughton.
3   Meek (1988).
4   Vygotsky, L. (1962) *Thought and Language*, Cambridge, MA: MIT Press.
5   Watson, V. (1992) 'The possibilities of children's fiction', in M. Styles, E. Bearne and V. Watson (eds), *After Alice*, London: Cassell.

Chapter 3

From Minnie the Minx to Little Lord Fauntleroy

Understanding character in fiction

Chris Doddington

Minnie the Minx is the archetypal mischief-maker, creating havoc with her feline ally Chester wherever they go. In the 1996 *Beano Annual*, Minnie's 'A–Z of Minxing' gives us E for the Egg Minnie throws at Dad's head, and F for Fury when he sees red. Fights occur, suits are reduced to rags and manure is traipsed across carpets, so that Minnie is acknowledged as the No. 1 pest and worn out from a wonderful day full of 'excellent minxing in every way', falls blissfully asleep under a large picture of Dennis the Menace. Memories of Minnie as a baby reveal Dad's dreadful premonition: 'Gasp! She's going to be a real monkey this one!'; and there are many stories of Minnie to confirm that this has come true.

Minnie appeals to children by behaving badly without a shred of remorse, but with the security that her actions cause no lasting harm to anyone, including herself. From a very young age children can be quite aware that this is a character in fiction – real life is different. Nevertheless, conscious that children can learn a great deal from text, the watchful moralist in the creator of the stories ensures that Minnie sometimes gets 'paid back' – by getting a good washing or by having to make some repair to the damage she has done. Like all serialised stereotypes, Minnie never changes: punishment cannot discourage her and without fail she bounces back with an irrepressible relish for creating mayhem and mischief. Children can rely on her to shock and delight them by her bossiness and her audacious behaviour.

At the other end of the moralising spectrum, the stereotypical 'good child' is always rewarded and, like angelic Cedric in Frances Hodgson Burnett's *Little Lord Fauntleroy*, finds fortune and fame as just desserts for her or his fine, loving and kindly nature. Characters in fiction have a long history of being used to teach by implication the virtues, and in the past this is undeniably why some texts have been judged edifying and therefore suitable as school texts. However, this is only part of the story of why children should read such texts; and to understand where the educational value of character lies we need to dig a little deeper.

What is character?

Literature often endears itself to us and becomes memorable through its characterisations. We relish the larger-than-life qualities of characters in Dickens, and painfully recognise the inner turmoil of Hamlet or the foolish arrogance of King Lear. In children's literature, characterisation is what makes a book a classic. Think of Alice, Huckleberry Finn or Anne of Green Gables. Children often adopt the personalities of the characters they read about: for instance, a friend's 6-year-old child announced 'I am Julian', having just finished the first chapter of *Five on a Treasure Island* (Blyton: 1942); and it is not unusual to see fictional characters embodied, alive and in good form, in children around school. Pocahontas and Sonic the Hedgehog relive their adventures in the playground, and jostle for space alongside Harry Potter and his wizard friend or cartoon characters from media texts such as *Sky Dancers* or *Rugrats*. A brief survey of children in one primary school revealed that spies, Mathilda and Mildred the Worst Witch were popular characters to play in role, and one boy poignantly said that whenever he was not included in the lunch-time football games he played on his own, and usually became the Tin Man from *The Wizard of Oz*.

> The 'knowing' of characters in books is a vital part of early literacy and is established from a young age. Indeed, many children will be familiar with characters from television such as Postman Pat and Fireman Sam. They come to school with a plurality of readings of such characters, for example from viewing (either the television programme or video), books, comics, toys marketed under franchise, puzzles, T-shirts, trainers and all kinds of stationery. This lays down a pattern of expectation which can rapidly transfer into reading behaviour.
>
> (Daniels 1996: 45)

There is a level at which most children seem to have no difficulty understanding characters from fiction. However, it is important that as teachers we are clear exactly *what* understanding we are fostering in schoolchildren. In everyday terms, 'character' refers to the collective personal qualities that distinguish one person from another, but the significant characteristics of individuals are often states of mind or moral dispositions. We describe others as 'kind', 'generous', 'cheerful' or 'courageous', and yet these qualities clearly differ from other attributes such as height ('tall') and physique ('thin'). Many of our significant characteristics are invisible to the eye, and we have to build up our impressions and understanding of someone from what they say or do – we learn to infer someone's character from behaviour. Part of the excitement of literature lies in the fact that fictional characterisation can be fuller and much more explicit than in life. Characteristics can be both described *and* inferred from a person's appearance, choice of words, actions, dialogue and interaction with others. This means that an author can build slowly during the course of a novel, describing, giving examples and selecting what is important for us to know about someone's character:

> One of the things which always delighted the people who made the acquaintance of his young lordship was the sage little air he wore at times when he gave himself up to conversation; combined with his occasionally elderly remarks and the extreme innocence and serious-ness of his round childish face, it was irresistible. He was such a handsome, blooming, curly headed little fellow, that when he sat down and nursed his knee with his chubby hands, and conversed with much gravity, he was a source of great entertainment to his hearers. Gradually Mr Havisham had begun to derive a great deal of private pleasure and amusement from his society.
>
> (Hodgson Burnett 1886: 45)

An author paints characters from a pallet of impressions, language, appear-ance, thoughts, actions and motives, choosing the setting and timing of revelations with care. The visual depiction of Minnie the Minx as ungainly and her incessant plans for mischief are sufficient to make her character perfectly clear. On the other hand, the slow revelation of the charac-ter Goggle-Eyes is artfully 'prismed' initially through Kitty's eyes, in Anne Fine's *Goggle-Eyes* (1990). Babe is introduced in Dick King-Smith's *The Sheep–Pig* (1995) by sound as merely a squealing pig who begins to endear himself to stolid Mr Hoggett simply by becoming quiet in his hands. The transition from mere animal to character does not occur until well into Chapter 2, with the spoken words: 'I'm a Large White.'

However authors choose to introduce and reveal character, the inten-tion is to allow readers to meet others who are necessarily outside of their own life-contexts. Characters give us rich experience of existences different from our own.

All human life

Much of literature centres on characters, their interactions and relation-ships. Fiction often conjures particular communities and cultures, yet however alien a context may be to us, good texts will have universal elements – things we can identify with or recognise. The poverty of the Little Match Girl in Hans Christian Andersen's well-known tale is unlikely to reflect our own experience, but the decision to spend precious resources for the sake of a moment's pleasure is an all too common human foible readers can recognise. The Little Match Girl's sense of cold, loss and neglect resonate with similar feelings that we can sense from our own experience.

The evocative illustration by Ralph Steadman in Naomi Lewis' version of the tale complements the text beautifully and enhances our powers of empathy to allow emotional connection with this character and her predicament:

> Her hands were quite numb with cold. A match flame would be such a comfort. Oh if only she dared to strike one match, just one. She took one and struck it against the wall – crrritch! How it cracked and blazed! What a lovely warm clear flame, just like a little candle!
>
> (Lewis 1988: 62)

When children encounter characters in fiction, then, they can learn about diversity of lifestyle, attitudes, behaviour and motives, the range of which would be impossible to encounter in the reality of their day-to-day existence. However, mere diversity and number of encounters do not ensure depth of understanding. Children need to be active in their reading by considering how attitude, behaviour and motive interact with events and context in order to develop understanding. This is where the writer's art of selecting ways to conjure a character in text, and the teacher's role of fostering appreciation of that art, are important.

Creating plays, stories and poems involves the weaving of characters within contexts and narratives. Selection serves to convey meaning as succinctly as possible and gives coherence and direction which real-life encounters by their haphazard nature lack. The illustrated story *The Day of Ahmed's Secret* introduces to the reader a child in a country very different from Britain, and we learn about him as we follow him through a day in his life. This story, however, is much more than an exercise in 'shadowing' life in another culture. The reader is 'hooked' by the mystery of the very first line – 'Today I have a secret, and all day long my secret will be like a friend to me' – and is then reeled expertly through significant points of Ahmed's day that reveal who he is and allow the reader to come to care about him. Within a single page we share the rich tapestry of the bustling streets of Cairo through Ahmed's eyes and ears:

> All kinds of sounds, maybe every sound in the world, are tangled together: trucks and donkeys, cars and camels, carts and buses, dogs and bells, shouts and calls and whistles and laughter all at once.

We learn that Ahmed feels significant among the crowd:

> I have a sound, too, the sound my cart makes: Karink rink, karink rink rink. I know my sound helps to make the whole sound of the city, and it would not be the same without me.
>
> (Parry Heide and Heide Gilliland 1994: 5)

Like a friend, we follow Ahmed around, eager to hear the secret he tanta-
lisingly keeps reminding us of: 'Loudest of all to me today is the silent
sound of my secret, which I have not yet spoken' (ibid.).

Throughout the rest of the book we share his feeling of pride as he
competently carries the heavy bottles for delivery, his need for quiet time
in the middle of the day and his memories of the wise sayings of his father,
urging him on: 'Hurry to grow strong, Ahmed. . . . But do not hurry to
grow old.' The location features almost incidentally, both through tiny
personalised detail – 'First I try to knock the sand from my sandals' – and
through information remembered by Ahmed – 'He tells me that the great
desert presses against our city on one side, and the great river pushes against
it on the other.'

Not only does this give the setting for Ahmed's life experiences, but
serves to reveal his love and admiration for his father without explicitly
expressing the emotions. The text and the large, vibrant and evocative
illustrations work to enable the reader to understand and participate
in the whole family's pride and pleasure when Ahmed decides 'It is time
to tell my secret', and we discover that he has learnt to write his
own name.

This simple story, written in the form of a personal commentary on a
day in his life, allows us to meet Ahmed and learn about his life and his
central concerns in the space of perhaps ten minutes. We become attached
to Ahmed as a character in his own story, so that we care what happens
to him. In some ways literary texts with their unlimited opportunities for
characterisation are better resources for developing an understanding of
humanity than are real-life encounters. Literature can never replace life,
but part of the value of text in education is that children can concentrate
on discerning both 'good' and 'bad' traits in characters without facing the
danger, as they would in real life, of what is alien to them or the difficulty
of trying to interpret a flood of complex signs and signals. Children can
remain cosily shielded from harm and yet have intimate encounters with
evil in a beguiling form:

> In person he was cadaverous and blackavized, and his hair was dressed
> in long curls, which at a little distance looked like black candles, and
> gave a singularly threatening expression to his handsome countenance.
> His eyes were of the blue of the forget-me-not, and of a profound
> melancholy, save when he was plunging his hook into you, at which
> time two red spots appeared in them and lit them up horribly.
>
> (Barrie 1906: 64)

Thus text is prized, in part, because it can give the child reader an encounter
with character that is *safe* because it has been partially digested, by being
'art-formed' into fiction.

In the words of the Bunyip – 'What am I?'[1]

Learning about others' lives extends our knowledge of the world and its people, though getting to know others as friends, colleagues or partners requires more than observation or analysis of their behaviour. In real life, our direct knowledge and awareness of people is developed through inter-action. We receive impressions and information, but we also actively draw on our minds, using our own thoughts and experiences, in attempting to understand and make sense of other persons and their actions.

This process can be seen at work in our feelings of familiarity towards famous people whom we never actually meet. We might all 'receive' the same images of or commentaries on various political or media individuals, but the sense we as individuals make of them will differ because of the personal values and experiences through which we interpret what is presented to us. The public response to the death of the Princess of Wales indicated the powerful sense in which people felt they personally 'knew her'. We perhaps recognise the characteristics of these people precisely because we interpret their actions and images and engage our own values and experiences in thinking about them, therefore feeling that we 'under-stand' them. This may be because their behaviour reflects or throws into relief our own concerns and, as with real acquaintances, their words or actions challenge or refine our values and life experiences.

It is in this sense that, as the philosopher Charles Taylor explains, we clarify our own identity through interaction with others.

> There is no way we could be inducted into personhood except by being initiated into a language. .... So I can only learn what anger, love, anxiety, the aspiration to wholeness, etc., are through my and others' experience of these being objects for *us*, in some common space.
>
> (Taylor 1989: 35)

Taylor suggests that everything would be confusion for a child 'without the conversations which fix this language' (ibid.: 36).

This form of conversation is similar to what can occur when we encounter characters in literary texts. Young children can become familiar with the interplay of their own feelings of frustration and anger as, for example, they identify with or distinguish their own characteristics and behaviour from Angry Arthur (Oram and Kitamura 1982). Similarly sensing that one's voice is not heard, nor one's presence fully felt can become concrete and link one with others whose similar experiences are depicted in literary form – for example in *Not Now, Bernard* (McKee 1980). I discover that someone else has had the feelings that I have felt but never articulated. I under-stand more about myself by recognising Bernard's predicament. Delving into the motives and fictional lives of others will therefore help children reflect upon their own feelings, behaviours and values, helping to define their identity. Learning to compare and distinguish myself from the motives, feelings and values of others helps to form and articulate my own characteristics and therefore who I am.

This incidental definition of self comes not only by identification with characters thus similar to ourselves: being imaginatively immersed in the existence of another liberates readers from their own existence and from themselves. While we are reading we can enter another time, another place, and 'feel' for characters who do not share our values and perhaps are quite unlike us. Our understanding grows through self-forgetfulness. It is in this sense that the author Jill Paton Walsh claims that literature offers us 'parole from the prison of the self' and reading becomes a:

> self-expanding, self-multiplying, self-dethroning process [that] can only be good for us; it is unambiguously good in the way that sight is better than blindness when you have to make your way in the world.
>
> (Paton Walsh 1996: 289)

Learning to be good

A. S. Byatt, in a 1992 seminar addressing the matter of the place of literature in public libraries, remarked:

> One of my greatest moments of moral recognition was when I read about Emma being rude to Miss Bates and realising that she had done something unpardonable and had hurt somebody. This struck at my soul and I have never been the same since.
>
> (Quoted in Standish 1997: 46)

Philosophers of education such as Paul Standish and Carole Cox (1997) have argued that powerful lessons in moral values are undoubtedly learnt from literature. We might assume that these are most efficiently taught explicitly, such as in the form of fairy story or fable, but as A. S. Byatt indicates in the passage quoted above, some of our most significant values are formed as we follow descriptions of the actions of characters which were not written primarily to teach us what being 'good' means. A story should not be valued merely as an instrument for inculcating values. Later in the contribution by Jill Paton Walsh cited above, an affliction particular to writers of children's texts described in terms of 'a lack of trust in the audience, a terrible anxiety that they won't understand art. If you show them something cruel happening, you are afraid that they will think you are in favour of cruelty' (Paton Walsh 1996: 284).

We can undoubtedly gain wisdom by considering what should be done in our own or someone else's moral quandary, but we do not automatically come to mimic the values or behaviour of characters we see on stage or read about in books.

> My niece . . . began again her normal practice of watching 'Neighbours' and telephoning her friends and talking to them for two hours about what the people in 'Neighbours' ought to have done. You can argue that this is exactly the same sort of moral discovery as my discovery that Emma had done something terrible. . . .
>
> (Byatt in Standish 1997: 46)

A. S. Byatt goes on to explain why *Emma* might offer more subtle moral insight than a TV soap, but is convinced that both high literature and popular media text can extend understanding of what it means to be human. She concludes: 'I think that my niece needs both; she needs *Emma* and she needs to talk like crazy to her friends about what the characters from "Neighbours" should have done' (ibid.).

Moral predicaments that catch our real concern are always concrete and particular. The beauty of a character in literature facing a moral predicament is that the reader can share that particularity and understand the problem from the inside without having to live through it. This gives the author tremendous power, but it is also the reason why Paton Walsh warns authors against the evangelising stance, emphasising that the reader must experience a character or a situation *directly*, 'unpestered and unobstructed' by the author's overt personal values. Children can see why and how *Burglar Bill* (Ahlberg 1977) exchanges his occupation of crime for that of a baker, but they see this by attending to Burglar Bill himself, not the moralising voice of the author. In *The Sheep–Pig* (King-Smith 1995), Fly the sheepdog, is rude to sheep but learns how to control her feelings, curb her prejudice and be polite when the need becomes great enough. We do not learn *about* all this; instead we feel the strength of Fly's effort and the warmth of her discovery alongside her, rather than direct from the author himself.

> Somehow Fly controlled her anger at the creature's stupidity. I must know what happened, she thought . . .
>
> 'Please,' she said once more in a voice choked with the effort of being humble, 'could you be kind enough to tell me what happened this morning?' . . .
>
> Listening, for the first time ever, to what the sheep were actually saying, Fly could hear individual voices competing to make themselves heard, in what was nothing less than a hymn of praise. . . . What a sense of relief flooded over her as she heard and understood the words of the sheep! It had been sheep-worriers, after all! And her boy had come to the rescue! He was not the villain, he was the hero!
>
> (King-Smith 1995: 86–7)

Character as art

When we look together with children at character in text, we are helping them learn how to piece together the jigsaw of narrative, action and description, so that a question like 'What kind of a person is Toad?' can be followed by 'How do we know he is impetuous?' Helping children understand how the author forms character in text is one vital aspect of initiating children into how the basic form of a text is constructed.

To develop this kind of awareness of text is essential, for it is the basis of a form of critical, analytical thinking which allows the reader to operate objectively with the text, learning to stand back and reason about the ways a text 'works'. Seeing the mechanics or pattern of character depiction in a text is to begin to critically evaluate text. This empowers children in their own writing by giving them a process for consciously structuring their ideas into literary form. Nevertheless, an analytical approach should also allow for poetic experience of the text and the characters found within it. Real appreciation of character draws on a blend of conceptual and emotional depth of experience. An engagement of the reader's feelings or interest is essential to allow emotional response, so that personal meanings can crystallise alongside the intellectual enquiry that is traditionally the basis for literary criticism. Many people look back on their own studies in English literature, at secondary school and beyond, with tales of being alienated by difficult texts which had appeared arid until there was a breakthrough to personal meaning. Eighteen months into her A-level course, my daughter has just discovered the vibrantly complicated characters of Eve, Adam and Satan in Milton's *Paradise Lost* (1667), as they speak deeply and skilfully to her own feelings of pride, self worth and temptation.

If personal response to character is important in reading, then in what sense should teachers teach for 'response'. Should we assume that children will respond if only a suitably relevant text can be found? If this were the whole story then the idea of developing personal response to characters would require little teaching, just good selection. However, it is clear that, while appropriate selection is a crucial feature of good teaching, enabling children to express the richness of their responses is equally skilful. Many of our so-called 'natural' responses to the arts are in fact culturally learned. All hearing babies physically respond to sound, but to jiggle or tap in response to the particular kinds of sounds that verge on dance is a learned response because they grow up in communities in which people commonly move their bodies to music and rhythm. Similarly it is not innate ability that leads us to recognise the tiny two-dimensional figures in a photograph as people. We have to learn this. Some of the specific abilities associated with responding to characters – the ability to imagine ourselves in the shoes of another person, the ability to suspend disbelief so that we 'feel' for actors on stage or screen, and understand that they do not actually die or suffer – should therefore be seen as *learned* responses which teachers can deliberately develop and enhance.

Understanding character in fiction will thus involve an emotional invest-ment from the reader. This allows a reader to reflect not only on the predicaments within the fiction but on their own values and experiences of life. Teachers are responsible for helping to develop responsive abilities, but also for encouraging children to be *disposed* towards this way of approaching character. How can teachers best help children respond and develop attitudes to reading that will encourage them to want to place themselves emotionally alongside characters in a text? Teachers will have their own range of strategies for achieving this degree of involvement with character, but I now want to look more closely at one rich but perhaps rather under-used method.

Stepping into someone else's shoes

Anyone who spends time observing young children in nurseries and infant classrooms cannot fail to appreciate how easily some children become absorbed in the imaginative act of pretending to be someone else. There are many accounts of the value of this kind of spontaneous play and, recently, accounts of the value of extending the learning potential of this activity through adult structures and intervention. If teachers are seeking ways to truly 'involve' children's thinking about character by having them speaking and behaving 'as if' they were someone else, then imaginative role play has an obvious potential use. Indeed, using role play to develop speaking and listening skills is frequent suggested, though somewhat seldomly employed:

> Pupil's skills in Speaking and Listening are generally good. They listen well, describe experiences clearly and discuss their work confidently. However, drama, especially role play and improvisation, is underused in many schools as a way of strengthening pupils' skills in speaking and listening.
>
> (Woodhead 1998: 8)

Imaginative role play is valued in part because it involves children emotion-ally, making 'dilemmas' or problems real enough to be meaningfully con-sidered and acted upon. A child's language resources are sometimes drawn deeply upon to create worlds in which he or she is someone else. Using drama, then, to involve children in the underlying tensions and interaction of characters within a story is a useful device to bring the story to life and help children understand or identify with fictional characters, and then reflect back on their own feelings and values. Take as an example a dramatic exchange with 6-year-olds, based on the story of Sleeping Beauty and led by the teacher in role as the bad fairy. Here children interview the bad fairy about what occurred between her and the king and queen prior to the birth of the princess. Children in groups might create and depict a tableau of the event or series of events that originally persuaded the fairy to give her a curse. This activity offers some understanding of motive and seeks explanation behind 'bad' or immoral actions. If the drama works well, emotions such as resentment, revenge and sympathy for the innocent can be discussed on the basis of a highly imaginative and involving experience for the children, yet from within the safety of a fictional context.

Drama arising directly from text is perhaps less familiar in primary schools than the form of improvised story-line drama just outlined, but in principle it offers similar value. Using the words and contexts drawn directly from a text involves 'pretending to be' someone else in a less open-ended form of drama at first glance may seem a more limited and less creative activity than structured role play. One argument frequently forwarded for not using written narratives and dialogue with young children is that text is pre-formed to such an extent that it provides too defined a narrative, restricting the mental space available for children to become involved, make authentic decisions, use their imagination and their own spontaneous language. If these attributes are what make other forms of drama so educationally valuable then children trying to operate as 'pre-ordained' characters are likely to appear wooden. It is argued that acting out text on this basis provides at best a vehicle for building confidence or a rather contrived but experiential introduction to our literary or cultural inheritance. I wish to challenge this particular view by looking at why practical drama which uses text is a useful way to teach children about understanding character.

Character speech

Poems, stories and novels, as well as plays for primary schoolchildren, often have extensive written dialogue which can be lifted directly from the page to be read or memorised as the basis for drama. The first step is to be clear what can be gained by physically acting these words over and above a static reading of the text.

The physical change that occurs when silent reading becomes reading aloud is a good place to begin. If a reader physically feels the words resonate within the body and at the same time hears what they say he or she is thereby brought emotionally closer to the text. Many argue that this increases the enjoyment and helps bring the character 'to life'. The assumptions being made here can be explained and are extended in writings by R. G. Collingwood. He argues strongly for an overall conception of language which stresses the essential physicality of speech. Unlike theories which view words as labels for what pre-exists, Collingwood's suggestion (which is echoed by many more recent philosophers of language) is that our spoken words are *not* static reflections of emotions or ideas already existing within our minds. Articulation or speaking our thoughts is the means by which we actually create or constitute the meaning and emotional subtlety and depth to our lives. Language for Collingwood is not just words but is best understood as 'total bodily gesture', so that our whole bodily expression helps to form what we think and who we are, not just our spoken words.

If there is any truth in this, then the significance of saying the words of a character aloud grows. Spoken words in the text are explicitly creating the character of those speaking, and when the words are 'acted', this process can become even clearer for the 'actor'. The spoken words on the page are suggestive of the emotions, motives and life experience of a character, and if we are aiming for readers to 'interact', they need to invest their own experiences and understandings to flesh out the character. My suggestion here is that physically acting as opposed to merely reading the character's part requires movement, sound and gesture as well as words, and is a demanding activity. The physical articulation of the names and the speech patterns given for giants in the play *The BFG*, for instance, calls upon children to take an imaginative leap from experience of their own body into the body and life of someone very different to them:

BLOODBOTTLER:	'Tis the witchy hour. And I is starveling!
FLESHLUMPEATER:	I is starveling rotten too!
GIANTS:	And I! And I! And I! And I!
BONECRUNCHER:	Let us go guzzle human beans!
CHILDCHEWER:	Let us flush bunk to England!
GIZZARDGULPER:	England is a luctuous land and I is fancying a few nice little English chiddlers!

(Wood 1993: 76)

The musicality and rhythm of the words cry out to be expressed with the gesture and posture that the words imply. Different children will be responsive in different ways – some being drawn towards movement or sound, others finding words more supportive as they 'transform' into giants. However the main educational point here is that physical involvement makes different, and some would say extensive, personal demands on children as they 'become' a fictional character, and this is likely to enhance understanding.

If *total bodily gesture* is involved in expressive language, as Collingwood suggests, progression in children's language development must involve increases in awareness, sensitivity and refinement in the visual, auditory and physical as well as oral aspects of speech. By becoming embodiments of the words, gestures and actions of a character, and by acting out the relationships and events suggested in a text, children gain the opportunity to be more emotionally involved and more expressive. They may also gain a deeper understanding of the feelings and values of those embroiled in the predicament of the workhouse in, say, *Oliver Twist* through the multidimensional physicality of drama experience. If we accept the concept and significance of 'total bodily gesture', then using drama will be important also for giving children the opportunity to develop awareness of vital aspects of spoken language in its fullest sense.

It is important to stress that merely standing and moving about while speaking does not constitute the quality of engagement I have outlined here. It is rather the physicality which drama provokes, and which in turn is enhanced by the quality of emotional engagement I have suggested, that we should aim at as teachers. This means that if we are to use drama as a way of understanding character in text, there is need of a quality of imaginative engagement akin to the best examples of children's spontaneous role play. For the teacher, this means that care is needed to set up a context with children that holds their interest and supports them in their physical characterisations. Imaginative enactment based closely on text offers a depth of understanding of character that can serve both literature and the wider educational demands of inculcating values.

Conclusion

This chapter has tried to analyse and exemplify what can be meant by understanding character in text. Thinking about the underlying purposes of exploring character in fiction helps to explain the need for an imaginative quality of engagement with text. I have tried to suggest the importance and the means of allowing children to connect with and at the same time reflect on character. Following on from these ideas there are questions that teachers may like to consider as they evaluate the experiences children have with character:

- Are the children really engaged with this character?
- Have the children been able to imagine the dilemmas, the predicaments, or the emotions involved and have they therefore been able to draw on their own life experience to reflect upon and understand this character?
- Can they generalise, considering what someone should do in a situation like this?
- Can they both make connections and reflect back on their own values because of this activity?

None of these questions is simple to answer, and they hardly lend themselves to paper and pencil assessment in the primary school. However they signal the valuable professional judgements that teachers have to make when educating children through character. If there are any doubts as to the vital role the teacher should play in this process, then the following statement made in 1996 by a New York teacher serves as a reminder of the great value that can be envisaged for the teaching of literature:

> I was supposed to be a welfare statistic. . . . It is because of a teacher that I sit at this table. I remember her telling us one cold, miserable day that she could not make our clothing better; she could not provide us with food; she could not change the terrible segregated conditions under which we lived. She could [however] introduce us to the world of reading, the world of books, and that is what she did.
>
> What a world! I visited Asia and Africa. I saw magnificent sunsets; tasted exotic foods; I fell in love and danced in wonderful halls. I ran away with escaped slaves and stood beside a teenage martyr; I visited lakes and streams and composed lines of verse. I knew then that I wanted to help children do the same things, I wanted to weave magic . . .
>
> (Clements 1998: 26)

Learning to understand character may not always be magical for all children; but if at all possible it should be. With the rich and ever-growing literature resources available for teachers, and a clear view about the journey we want children to undertake, perhaps it is possible to weave more magic for even more children.

Note

1   Wagner, J. and Brooks, R. (1975) *The Bunyip of Berkeley's Creek*, London: Picture Puffin.

References

Ahlberg, A. (1977) *Burglar Bill*, London: Heinemann.

Barrie, J. M. (1906) *Peter Pan*, London: Puffin [1988].

Blyton, E. (1942) *Five on a Treasure Island*, London: Hodder & Stoughton.

Clements, S. (1998) 'Book Review of "Whose school is it, anyway?" by Kathryn Riley', *Improving Schools*, Vol. 1, No. 3, pp. 26–32.

Cox, C. (1997) 'A moral fix', in Smith and Standish (eds), *Teaching Right and Wrong*.

Daniels, J. (1996) 'Is a series reader a serious reader?', in Styles, Bearne and Watson (eds), *Voices Off*.

Fine, A. (1990) *Goggle-Eyes*, London: Puffin.

Hodgson Burnett, F. (1886) *Little Lord Fauntleroy*, Oxford: Oxford University Press [1993].

King-Smith, D. (1995) *The Sheep–Pig*, London: Puffin.

Lewis, N. (1988) *The Flying Trunk and Other Stories from Andersen*, London: Arrow Books [1986].

McKee, D. (1980) *Not Now, Bernard*, London: Andersen Press.

Milton, J. (1667) *Paradise Lost: Books I–X*, London: Penguin [1968].

Oram, H. and Kitamura, S. (1982) *Angry Arthur*, London: Andersen Press.

Parry Heide, F., Heide Gilliland, J. (1994) *The Day of Ahmed's Secret*, London: Cassell [1995].

Paton Walsh, J. (1996) 'The masks of the narrator', in Styles, Bearne and Watson (eds), *Voices Off.*

Smith, R. and Standish, P. (eds) (1997) *Teaching Right and Wrong*, Stoke-on-Trent: Trenham Books, Ltd.

Standish, P. (1997) 'Fabulously absolute', in Smith and Standish (eds), *Teaching Right and Wrong.*

Styles, M., Bearne, E. and Watson, V. (eds) (1996) *Voices Off. Texts, Contexts and Readers*, London: Cassell.

Taylor, C. (1989) *Sources of Self. The Making of Modern Identity*, Cambridge: Cambridge University Press [1992].

Wood, D. (1993) *Roald Dahl's The BFG*, London: Puffin.

Woodhead, C. (1998) *Chief Inspector of Schools' Annual Report for 1997*, London: DfEE.

Chapter 4

Juvenile leads

Nick Warburton

When I started to think about plays for children, I found myself remembering two incidents which seemed to have some bearing on the subject: the first time I deliberately made people laugh, and my attempt to produce Shakespeare with 10-year-olds.

I was in the second-year juniors at Roding Lane, Woodford, when Miss Forester asked us to form groups – an adventure in itself in those days, when a child could hide behind whole-class teaching. She told us to improvise a story for the rest of the class. I believe our story was something to do with a hut in the mountains, though the twists and turns of the plot have long since faded from memory. I can, however, recall with some clarity the moment when a certain bit of spontaneous business occurred to me. I decided that, if I contrived to trip over and plunge my head in the wastepaper bin by Miss Forester's desk, it might go down well with the audience. It did. The bin was dark green and had pencil shavings in it. I can still clearly picture the shavings and hear the laughter of the other children. It is possible that, with my head in the bin, the laughter was somewhat amplified, but all the same it was a sweet moment. What I had achieved, of course, was a fairly cheap laugh, and it would be stretching the point to classify this as a literary experience. Nevertheless, it did have some significance, and, though I was unaware of it at the time, through it I learned several things. I had learned something about dramatic events, the things that happen in acting spaces which convey meaning or emotion in ways that the printed word cannot. It taught me also something about the relationship between a live audience and the performer. Above all it boosted the confidence of a child who had achieved no great success in other areas of the curriculum.

The second incident occurred many years later, during my early experience of teaching. I divided my class of 10-year-olds into groups and asked them to present scenes from A *Midsummer Night's Dream*, *The Tempest*, *Julius Caesar*, *Macbeth* and *Hamlet*. It proved to be less straightforward than I had imagined – Christopher as Polonius never quite understood the perplexing line 'Take this from this if this be otherwise' – and, in retrospect, it seems obvious that it was a naive and foolhardy plan, unwieldy and unnecessarily full of headache and worry. Looking back, I know it was a mistake, but I am still inclined to think of it as a worthwhile mistake, and one inspired perhaps by what I had learned all those years ago at Roding Lane. It was not without its benefits for the young performers. The children gained some sort of experience of Shakespeare and so, perhaps, lost a little of the fear which is often associated with his plays. When children put on a play, they can cope with texts which are initially perplexing, and with language richer and more strange than they are likely to meet elsewhere. They learn and recite it, live with it for some considerable time and ponder the motives of the characters, so that what is at first opaque gradually becomes clear – 'daylight and champain', as Malvolio says. I am sure also that being one of those murdering Caesar or a witch mixing an evil brew helped to build the children's confidence and gave them the chance to identify with another persona. Acting in a play is, as someone once memorably described it, not simply 'shouting in the evenings'. It allows one to experience the release of all sorts of emotions, and to know something of what it is like to be in another person's shoes.

With these incidents in mind, I was prompted to ask two questions about plays for children. What do we mean by 'a play'? And how can we help children to write one?

What do we mean by a play?

The National Curriculum dictates that the Writing component should include dialogues, narrative and drama scripts. This is less straightforward than it sounds. Drama scripts, for instance, are not essentially different from dialogue and narrative; being usually a blend of the two of which the sum should be greater than the parts. In fact, I am not convinced that we always know what we mean when we ask children to 'write a play'.

Our thinking on the subject tends to be muddled. For a start, there is sometimes confusion between *doing drama* and *putting on a play*. Clearly the two overlap – my head-in-the-bin early experience was doing drama – but they are really separate activities. What we explore when we do drama is very often ourselves – our thoughts and feelings, the way we move and speak. We deal with these things, too, when we put on a play, but here the focus is different: those aspects of self – thoughts, feelings, movement and speech – are used to serve a text, and that text contains characters. Instead of examining the self, in a play we attempt the equally valuable but different task of presenting *the other*.

We encounter another sort of confusion if our definition of a play is not precise enough. If we think of a play merely as, for example, 'a story told in dialogue', we are giving only a partial definition. When we watch Rowan Atkinson as Mr Bean or a Buster Keaton film, or television adverts, what we are watching are plays, even though they may have little or no dialogue. There is more to telling a story using the format of a play than filleting out the prose to isolate the speech.

The matter can be clarified a little by asking ourselves – and indeed asking our children – what differences there are between a play and a story told in prose. A play is seen or heard and a story is read; a story needs only a reader to make it work whereas a play requires performers and people to support them; you can read a story when you like, and take as long as you like, but a play takes place over a given period of time. These attempts to pin down a definition make us aware that plays differ significantly from stories, and that it is no easy task to write one. (Many, though not all, successful novelists have made unsuccessful attempts to write a play. On the other hand, dramatisations by playwrights of works by Henry James or Joseph Conrad, for instance, have been more successful than any of the attempts those great writers made to write plays themselves.) And yet we are charged with persuading children to write drama scripts.

While it is wise to acknowledge the difficulties we are likely to meet in writing plays, we should not feel daunted by those difficulties. Some can be overcome by getting children to read plays – and to read them *properly*. On the whole, people rarely read plays, and this is partly because plays need to be read in a way different from that required by prose narratives. A play script is really a set of instructions, and to read one is, in some respects, like reading a music score. If we are tempted to skip the stage directions and read only the dialogue – and that is what usually happens – we fail to get the complete picture. We miss those parts of the drama which are not conveyed through words. Reading a play requires a distinctive comprehension: to appreciate it properly we have to read a play as if we mean to perform it. In fact, we have to create a kind of performance of it in our imaginations. Only then will we be able to understand all it has to offer – the story, the dialogue and those essentially dramatic events that carry so much of its meaning.

It is true that the dramatic elements of a play are sometimes to be found in the dialogue. A boy stands before his father, who says: 'Now, be honest. Did you chop down the cherry tree?' Both the question and the boy's answer constitute a dramatic event, a kind of turning-point or a moment of significance. There are many occasions, though, when the dramatic event is not found in what the characters are saying but in what they are doing (or not doing) – 'head-in-the-bin' moments, if you like. In *Richard III*, Richard of Gloucester offers Lady Anne a sword so she can take revenge on him for the murder of her husband. Lady Anne refuses to take it. Both the offer and the refusal are dramatic events. At the end of *The Cherry Orchard* everyone except Firs, the old servant, leaves the Ranevskaya home, and this emptying of the stage is a dramatic event. Sound and light can also provide dramatic events. The sound of the axes on the Ranevskaya orchard is a dramatic event. So, in a less event way, is the gradual darkening of the garden outside of the room in which Harold Pinter's *Ashes to Ashes* takes place. In this case the event is subtle and unfolds during the course of the play: it is not like the momentary act of the offering of a sword, but nevertheless is part of what happens and has significance. Even costume changes can constitute events. Through several scenes in Alan Bennett's monologue *Soldiering On*, from *Talking Heads*, we see the speaker's costume becoming more dowdy as her circumstances worsen. Our recognition of these changes is part of our experience of the play.

So a play is usually a combination of dialogue, events, sound, light, setting, and so on. But even when we appreciate all this, we need still to distinguish the play's type. Many beginning writers produce what they call a play without having given much thought to its exact nature. They say: 'Well, it's a play, isn't it? You know, people put it on.' But a play can be put on the stage, or on film, or on the radio. Scripts for stage, film (or television) and radio are, indeed, all plays, but each will be a play with a particular emphasis. One key difference between these types of play is the way that they act on an audience. The audience for a stage play will probably be more committed (having paid for seats and bothered to turn up) than the audience for a television or radio play. The audience for a radio play, though it can be counted in hundreds of thousands, is, effectively, an audience of one: the radio playwright addresses a single listener who, through imaginative listening, makes a considerable contribution to the drama. Two people *listening* to the same play will create different pictures in their imaginations as a result of what each hears. The radio playwright must also write in a way that is specific to radio. (At the simplest level, this means that the usual directions for visual elements – lighting changes or costume notes, and many of the instructions for movement – are irrelevant.) Different techniques are required for writing radio, film and stage plays. This chapter's concern is not with considering these techniques themselves – one can learn about them by reading scripts specifically intended for radio, stage or film – but we do need to be aware of their varied requirements when we ask children to write a play.

Some time after I started writing, I submitted a play to a theatre company. It was a play for children, and it was, quite rightly, rejected because it was unworkable: it had over thirty characters, and all of them were important to the action and had something significant to say. Few theatre companies can afford to put on such an extravaganza. This was a naive mistake to make, but, looking back, I realise why I made it. I thought that plays for children formed a single category. Common sense should have told me that there were several categories – plays which children can see; those they can hear; those they can read; and those they can perform. (There is also, of course, a category of plays *about* children, which can sometimes be confused with plays for children.) It seems, therefore, a good idea to provide children with a variety of plays which engage them in these different ways – as readers, performers and audience.

How can we help children to become playwrights?

To become a playwright you must first understand what a play is and decide on the type of play you want to write. Then you will need to practise a number of skills specific to the creation of scripts. You will need to learn how to

- write dialogue
- write stage directions
- identify and then write dramatic events
- structure a play.

We need not worry too much about the creation of dramatic events and structure if we are teaching young children to write plays. These are comparatively abstract and sophisticated aspects of writing plays, and it's probably enough for us, as teachers, to recognise them when they do occur in what the children write. It would be asking rather a lot to expect young writers to attempt the sort of subtle lighting change Pinter uses in *Ashes to Ashes*. They are more likely to include momentary events – TIM TRIPS OVER THE BOX, for instance, or TIM PUTS HIS HEAD IN THE WASTE-PAPER BIN – and when they do, we can point this out and praise them for their instinctive dramatic expertise. If children do not write dramatic events – if their scripts are no more than dialogue – we can encourage them to 'make things happen', to give their audiences something to see as well as words to hear.

Structuring a play, which involves constructing and relating the scenes and acts which make up a play, is a complex business best dealt with when children have gained more experience of writing dialogue and stage directions. One can, however, point out the importance of making good and dramatic beginnings and endings, and say something about making sure that all the characters in a script are relevant to the plot. It might be counterproductive to go much further than that. Indeed, it is probably unwise to push children to write whole plays: it is challenging enough for them to write scenes – even scenes restricted to two or three characters. (You could, perhaps, ask them to write short scenes, individually or in small groups, which may subsequently be assembled into a complete script.)

Dialogue and stage directions, although they involve skills which can be developed to considerable levels of sophistication, are more concrete. Consequently there are certain things we can do to help children write them. If we are dealing with dialogue, we can get them to speak and listen to each other. We can get them to recognise how speech is different from conventional written English – that individual speakers have their own rhythms, their own little habits of hesitation, emphasis and repetition, very often their own vocabulary. Children can be asked to tune in to the strange and telling phrases people use when they talk, and to remember and note down odd snippets of conversation they hear in shops and the playground. By encouraging children to break up speech with questions, interruptions and misunderstandings, we can help them to write dialogue which reflects the rhythms of speech, the frustrations of communication and the individuality of the speakers.

The poor dialogue one sometimes reads in scripts often springs from two basic misconceptions on the part of the writer. One is that characters should say exactly what they want to say in uninterrupted chunks. The other is that everyone speaks in roughly the same way. A writer's failure to differentiate between characters can result in all of the characters sounding as if they speak with the same voice. Young playwrights – playwrights of any age, in fact – should learn how to write from different points of view and to find their characters' distinctive voices. One way of doing this is to ask them to write monologues. By writing for a single character, writers can more easily hear that character's voice. Once they have managed this, they can introduce a second character, very different from the first. Perhaps their second character will have a different background or experience, be older or younger. Perhaps he or she will fail to understand what has been said, will interrupt and ask questions, and have aims and intentions at variance with those of the first character.

Writing stage directions – or directions for the camera or microphone – is largely a matter of setting down instructions. A playwright must give the director and cast precise instructions about what he or she wants an audience to see or hear. This means thinking clearly about the setting of the play, the things that happen in it, the ways the lighting changes and the way sound and music are used. The writer must describe those things as simply and unambiguously as possible. The skills needed to write good stage directions – clarity of thought and simplicity of expression – are transferable: they provide excellent practice for non-dramatic writing, too. In fact, it is paradoxical that stage directions can sometimes read like poetry, simply because the writer is striving not for effect but rather to be clear and uncomplicated.

In conclusion

I believe it is important to give plays the attention they deserve and to find a proper place for them in the curriculum. Experience of a variety of plays can broaden children's literary understanding and help them to develop as writers in general. It can also enhance their appreciation of the plays they will probably encounter throughout their lives – stage and radio drama for a few, film and television for almost all. If they learn to write, read and perform plays they will almost certainly find a new awareness of themselves and others.

Chapter 5

Into the woods

Animating stories through drama

Andy Kempe

I am not a regular listener to *The Archers*, but in the early stages of preparing this chapter it seemed that every time I got into the car the programme was on the radio. The main storyline at the time concerned an attempt to mount a production of *A Midsummer Night's Dream* in Ambridge. Rather like the programme's fictional characters I became frustrated at how long this wretched project seemed to be taking. In one episode the actors who had volunteered or been cajoled into the production were at the end of their tether when the director announced that she was to do yet another workshop as part of the preparation. 'Why can't we just get on and learn the lines?' one amateur thespian asked a friend.

The saga reminded me of two comments concerning the reading of stories. Relating the findings of research into children's attitudes to class-readers, Andy Goodwyn (1994: 21) notes: 'A great many pupils stressed how dull they found it to "plod through books".' The other comment was made a few years ago by a year 9 pupil to a colleague who was teaching English in a comprehensive school: 'Why can't we just read good stories?' the boy asked. 'Why do we have to do all this stuff about issues?' It was an interesting question because the boy was a proficient reader who frequently made thoughtful and mature contributions to discussion. His awareness of current issues was beyond that of most of his peers, and he held strong opinions about things that others in his class simply never considered. It would seem that the boy was interested in issues but objected to the way in which they were explored, which appeared to him to be as an appendage to his encounter with the text rather than as integral to the encounter. Like the amateur actors of Ambridge, he did not see the point of working on *aspects* of the text which detracted from his central purpose – getting on with the business of interpreting the text for himself.

Taking another look at my initial scribblings for this chapter in the light of the introduction of the Literacy Hour, my attention was drawn to the opening sentence of *Framework for Teaching*, the National Literacy Project's statement on text work: 'At the text level . . . pupils' attention is directed to what the text is about' (1997: 11). The particular concern of this chapter is the way in which drama may be used in conjunction with picture-books with beginning readers in the primary school. It will not suggest that using drama is the only swift and efficient way of exploring storybooks and which leads to a full and deep understanding of what texts are about. Nor will it propose that drama can effectively replace the reading of good stories. It will, however, argue that drama can help draw pupils' attention to what texts are about without making them 'plod through' the issues or beating them over the head with what the teacher happens to think they are about. The practical ideas in this chapter embrace the concept espoused by the National Literacy Project that 'literacy' entails a broad definition, many aspects of which cannot be achieved by 'long sessions of reading to the class [or] class sessions of individual silent reading' (1997: 4). As Margaret Meek succinctly explains, literary competence involves more than 'simply recognizing words on the page' (1988: 10). She is persuasive in her account of the relationship between visual and verbal literacy: 'Television and books are allies. I don't believe that the one drives out the other. But we need to be clearer about the kinds of "reading" offered by both' (1988: 38).

Drama, entailing as it does the creation and interpretation of visual images, may, in this account, be seen as a natural resource on which to draw in order to develop a range of literary competences. Before exploring some practical examples of how this might be achieved it is necessary to consider the nature of stories in general in order to understand just what may be learnt by exploring 'what they are about'.

'All this stuff about issues'

There is an assumption that drama makes a great contribution to children's spiritual and moral development by its suitability as a medium to tackle social problems. Through role play children might, for example, be led to empathise with both the bully and the bullied, and so come to an understanding of bullying behaviour which will make them less likely to be culprits or victims. It is an assumption which has been unquestioningly accepted by some, while others have sought in vain for evidence of affective change resulting from such a direct approach. Reducing a full exploration of the polysemic nature of the art form to an investigation of the issues on which it draws for content is to deny the potency of the very symbolism that allows individuals to find resonance and meaning in it. The same could be argued for approaches to storybooks. It is a question of whether we believe that stories can somehow provide answers to issues or whether we consider them worth reading because they give new perspectives on the nature of the problems.

We are perhaps all familiar with incidents, real or fictionalised, in which someone who has a problem is told a story which serves to clarify what future action should be taken. A good example is afforded by Anne Fine's novel *Goggle-Eyes* (1989), in which a girl who is experiencing difficulties over her mother's new relationship draws strength from a story she is told by Kitty, the book's main character, who has been through a similar experience.

Steve Cockett (1997) argues that such an affective result comes about in one of two ways: either the story reinforces existing values and beliefs, and thus clarifies *possible* ways forward; or it subverts existing structures of belief and so offers new insights demanding a restructuring of those beliefs before any action is possible. In essence, Cockett argues, the difference here is between myth and parable. It is important to stress that the term 'myth' has a wider application than its use to refer to ancient stories and may be applied to any story which propagates the assumption that the human world is organised around a number of immutable truths. So, for example, the idea that the populace of ancient Greece may have been happy to accept that the seasons come around because of Persephone having to spend one-third of each year (wintertime) in Hades before she could return to the mortal realm to revitalise nature may seem to us charming yet bizarre, but in the absence of any more plausible explanation at the time at least the myth did no harm. In contrast, one may see how, by subscribing to the myth that Jews, Gypsies, Slavs and others are sub-human and therefore do not feel pain and emotion in the same way as true Aryans, the Nazis were able to treat them so abominably without, apparently, feeling any guilt.

Immersion in myth, then, may make things seem unproblematic. It is rather like simply accepting that, if *this* is the case, then *that* is the answer and there is no need to reflect further on the issue. Parable, however, exposes the fragility of myth. Whereas myth appears to deny interpretation, parable actively invites it and in so doing reveals the fact that we are always interpreting. Its function therefore is not to replace one myth with another in the attempt to solve problems, but to propose alternative lenses through which to view some problem and so know it better. A mark of 'good' literature may be that it allows readers to make links between the fictitious situation and their own experience. It is not that the fictitious situation is exactly the same as the reader's, but that the text offers the reader the possibility of melding the fiction into a frame through which they can view their own experiences. In this sense teachers may see working in parable as a fruitful means of encouraging children to think for themselves. By becoming more aware of the myths which threaten to govern our thoughts and actions, we may move on to negotiate our own specific solutions to specific problems rather than rely on generalisations and received wisdom.

Cockett goes on to make an extremely important point about parable when he reminds us that its power lies in its immediacy. With each retelling, a story, which at first may have been taken as a parable, moves inevitably towards myth in much the same way that once trendy expressions eventually become clichés. It becomes increasingly part of the received and accepted wisdom. Examples of this abound. Jack Zipes (1976, 1994) has illustrated how traditional folk tales, while initially acting as metaphors for real material conditions and thus acting effectively as parables, have, over the course of years, both informed and subsumed the changing values and beliefs of the societies in which they are told. Thus, the horror of Hansel and Gretel's experience of being abandoned by their stepmother, in order to make way for a new family and having to make their own way in life (presumably, argues Zipes, a material reality in times past), has its focus changed to the heroic deeds of the children. In times when the perception was that the reality of life could not possibly be quite so brutal, Hansel and Gretel's defeat of the witch, followed by their happy re-union with the father and stepmother, becomes an uplifting tale of Victorian family values. However, while such Disneyesque versions of traditional tales have entered our mythology (i.e. parents are basically good caring people), changing realities appear to ceaselessly contest such static formulations. In this way there is always a tension between the stories we hear and the stories we find ourselves a part of; drama is an art form which relies upon immediacy and the interplay between the real and the fictitious. As such, it has the capacity to explore such tensions and restore a parabolic dimension to tales which, because of their mythologisation (which may involve the 'watering down' of the narrative and the honing of the language used to convey it), may all too easily come to be seen as 'dull' and 'irrelevant'.

Monsters in masks

In his seminal work *The Uses of Enchantment*, Bruno Bettelheim (1976) argues against offering children only sanitised tales in which monsters always turn out to be friendly and nothing really bad ever happens to anyone. A good example of such a tale is Sleeping Beauty. Angela Carter's 1982 retelling of the tale restores much of the brutality of Perrault's seventeenth-century original. The overtones of sexual awakening had been dissipated in Victorian retellings, and those of us brought up on Disney's version are doubtless surprised to learn that the Prince had a mother who, after the marriage, plots to destroy both the Princess and her children by eating them. The notion which underpinned such sanitisation was that if children are not exposed to unpleasant images of the world they will be incapable of making their own, and as a result the world will be an altogether nicer place. Unfortunately, argues Bettelheim, such repression effectively dispossesses the child of an opportunity to learn how to deal with the monsters he or she already perceives to exist in the big wide world. More particularly, such a model misses 'the monster a child knows best and is most concerned with: the monster he feels or fears himself to be, and which sometimes persecutes him' (Bettelheim 1976: 120).

With the re-inclusion of these original elements, Angela Carter restores the possibility of interpreting the tale as a parable which allows children more points of reference for their own feelings. The restoration of monsters as metaphors dispels another myth which can be seen as destructive, and that is the myth of an essential self. There is a world of difference between the statements 'I am like that' and 'This is how I feel at the moment'. A part of Bettelheim's argument is that the structure, conventions and symbolic codes of folk tales allow children to recognise the transitory nature of their feelings. The creation and exploration of character in drama provides the opportunities for audiences to revel in the polysemic nature of our presence in the world. In other words, by giving fictional characters a physical and verbal presence we come to see not who or what we are, but who or what we may be if we so choose or if others demand it of us. Using drama to explore what stories are about helps us to understand what we are about: that is, we are not essential immutable selves with a fixed range of feelings and fixed ways of presenting those feelings, rather, we are beings with the capacity to cast ourselves as characters in many contexts and to play the character-type others have cast us in. To always submit unconsciously to the latter is akin to subscribing to a destructive fatalism; to recognise the possibility of casting ourselves as characters liberates us to take control of our own destiny as and when we choose.

In practice . . .

The two drama sessions described and analysed below tackle the issue of monsters. The sessions explore the nature of monsters and expose their metaphorical value. The picture-books used in the sessions work through parable, and this is made clear not only through the written text but through the illustrations also. The aim of the drama is, in each case, to draw the children's attention to the parable and so invite them to make a conscious interpretation of how the stories relate to their own experiences.

The first example is a workshop based on Jeanne Willis' *The Monster Bed* (1986). Here the 'monster' is, on the face of it, sanitised in a way of which Bettelheim might well disapprove. His name is Dennis and he is, when all is said and done, 'pretty cute'. Similarly, Dennis' mum, though depicted as physically a monster, palpably has all sorts of nice mumsy and seemingly unmonsterly attributes. However, there is another 'monster' in the story which is his mum's attitude to Dennis' fears and the actions she takes to try and assuage them.

Dennis is frightened of humans. Through this simple use of reversed perspective, children may come to see that while they might be frightened of the world, they themselves could well be frightening to other creatures. In the story, Dennis discovers to his horror that humans really do exist even though his mother has repeatedly told him they do not. The 'monster' here is the mother's immersion in a mythology which denies her child's perception and indeed experience. Perhaps I'm being a bit harsh on poor old mum here but, as you will see, by exploring the story through drama the children came to see that parents aren't monstrous by design, but can simply be wrong and make monstrous decisions. To illustrate a point made earlier, Dennis' mum, a metonym for all adults perhaps, is a character who is certain in her own knowledge – in this case, of the non-existence of humans. She regards Dennis, a metonym for all children, as an innocent. The tension, and indeed the fun of the story, arises because not only does Dennis reject being cast in this light but he turns out to be right.

The second example is Chris Van Allsburg's *The Widow's Broom* (1992). In this tale a witch crashes to earth when her broom is worn out. A widow helps her and is rewarded by the bequest of the witch's old broom which still has some magic left in it. The broom turns out to be very helpful to the widow, but its presence incenses her neighbours. This book, being explicitly concerned with witches, some teachers may initially consider unsuitable for use in the classroom. However, though I recognise and sympathise with concerns about the depiction of women as witches, in the case of this book I would argue that the strength of the narrative and the attitudes it explores (along with the stunning art work which subtly subverts stereotypical images of witches) offer sufficient justification for its use in schools. The drama makes use of a parable in which 'witchcraft' is a metaphor for anything alien; in this way the myths which govern the reactions of the villagers are exposed as manifestations of ignorance.

The Monster Bed

What follows is a brief account of a lesson undertaken at John Rankin Infants' School in Newbury. The class was made up of around twenty-six year 1 pupils, and this was their first experience of a structured drama. The class teacher was present as an observer and the lesson, which lasted about one-and-a-half hours, was led by myself with the assistance of Adam Fotheringham, a lecturer in drama at Newbury College of Further Education.

The session

The aim of the session was to encourage the children to recognise the possibility of seeing familiar stories in a new way. The structure drew on what we saw as the dynamic of Jeanne Willis' story, but consciously sought to challenge the children by asking them to both question the assumptions apparent in the tale and relate the dynamic to their own experience of traditional fairy tales. The content of the session is summarised here in nine stages.

1   The first two verses of *The Monster Bed* were read aloud:

> Never go down to the Withering Wood
> The goblins and ghoulies are up to no good.
> The gnomes are all nasty, the trolls are all hairy
> And even the pixies and fairies are scary.
>
> Oh, never go down there, unless you are brave,
> In case you discover the Cobbeldy Cave.
> For inside that cave which is gloomy and glum
> Live Dennis the monster and Dennis's mum.

The children were asked to suggest what other horrible things might be in the forest, and these were jotted down on a sheet of card. The rhythm and diction of these verses, along with the book's illustrations, presented the children with a number of exciting contradictions. While the written warning is clear, both the wood and Dennis look like fun! Such contradictions between words and images illustrate how children come to acquire specific, and indeed quite sophisticated, literary competence – an appreciation of irony. Asking them to suggest other 'horrible' things was an invitation to suggest the images they truly feared most in an environment which would accept and recognise them as horrible, while at the same time rendering them manageable. Their awareness of the ironic use of the word 'horrible' in this context was indicated by their gleeful responses to the invitation.

2   Individuals selected an idea from the noted suggestions, and made a sound and then a movement for it. Then, as a group, we created a 'soundscape' of the forest, varying the tone, volume and pace, and decided which was the most effective. Here again was a recognition of frightening images made manageable through the children's own manipulation of dramatic form.

3   The class then created a human maze to represent the woods. One teacher adopted the role of a small boy, and we recreated his experience of getting lost in the woods. Following this example, pupils were invited to go for a walk (with a teacher holding his or her hand) keeping their eyes shut to experience the 'horrible' atmosphere. The sounds and the movements really were felt to be rather scary, and the children relished presenting the things which frightened them. While this was, in itself, an empowerment, it was interesting to note the enthusiasm of the children volunteering for the 'Withering Wood' experience. The vicarious enjoyment of scarification to be found on the ghost train or in watching a horror film is, by its nature, ironic. The experience is only pleasurable because we know it is not real and we have some control over it. Having helped create this dramatic image

these pupils knew the limits and nature of its horrors! In this sense their literacy in a particular genre was extended.

4 The next three verses, which focus on Dennis' own fear of humans, were read out. One teacher adopted the role of Dennis' mum to explain to the class that she could understand Dennis' fear as some of the stories in a book (*The Little Monster's Book of Bedtime Tales*) bought for him by his aunty show humans as being pretty horrible. She used examples such as Goldilocks and Little Red Riding Hood, then invited the children to suggest other stories where the humans win their struggles with 'monsters' or animals. In role as the mother, the teacher constantly reinforced the notion that such stories were all nonsense as humans did not really exist.

In this deviation from the text the children were being invited to consciously adopt a set of beliefs which were clearly contrary to their own experience and knowledge. Their delight in adopting such a position might be interpreted as an indication of their desire, willingness and, indeed, ability to see things from a different perspective, especially one which contradicts the standard adult position that there are no monsters. At this point they were siding with a monster!

5 Working in small groups, the children chose a well-known story, trying to retell it to make sure they were clear about the events before preparing a presentation of the part of the story they thought might well frighten young beasts like Dennis.

This groupwork was carefully monitored. The teachers needed to give assistance with the challenge both of recalling the events of the story and of helping the children to see it from a new perspective. Some groups were encouraged to use still images; others decided to use a narrator. In some cases, the teacher narrated the story while the children showed the events.

The class briefly discussed how such stories might frighten young Dennis. Here, again, the teacher (in role as the mother) deliberately encouraged the children to share her perspective.

6 The teacher playing Dennis' mum recruited the children to help her get Dennis (played by a second teacher) into the bed. He eventually agreed to sleep under the bed, just as happens in the story. I can imagine situations in which the teacher might have preferred to feed this possibility to the children, but in this session it really did happen spontaneously – which gave the class an extra delight when they discovered, as another teacher read out the next part of the story, that was indeed the way Jeanne Willis had seen it.

7 Once Dennis had been persuaded to get under the bed the drama was stopped, following some spontaneous inter-play between two teachers in role, and the end of the story was read out along with an enactment

of the scene which ends with Dennis and the Boy running screaming around the room (much to the class's amusement!)

8   Up to this point the drama had concentrated on revealing the narrative and characters of the book. It was in the work that followed that pupils' attention was drawn to what the text is about, by exploring its themes and evaluating the behaviour of the characters. For this exploration, the class was asked to work in pairs, one child playing Dennis and the other playing Dennis' mum. Their brief was to improvise the conversation which took place the next morning, when Dennis tells his mum about the events of the previous night. Does she believe him? How does he convince her that humans really do exist?

9   Next the class was gathered together and asked to consider what had happened to Dennis. They were given the opportunity of 'speaking' to Dennis and his mum, having been reminded that they had earlier seen things from the mother's point of view, according to which stories about humans were nonsense. In the light of this what advice would they now give to the characters?

Through this discussion the real 'monster' of the story was revealed to be the way in which adults too readily dismiss children's fears simply because they are not adult fears. The fact that something may not exist in the 'real' world is not an effective antidote to the fear which occurs through imagining that it does exist. Though not expressed in these terms, the sentiment was illustrated through the pupils' becoming quite stern and insistent that Dennis' mum really should be more sympathetic to his beliefs in the future. The advice to Dennis was that he should stick to his guns and not always accept what adults say just because they are adults!

Follow-up tasks and ideas

From this initial drama session a number of different follow-up tasks were identified. As a result of this initial stimulus some children might simply be asked to recall elements of the narrative or to retell the story in their own written words or by group improvisation. Others might be offered the chance of drawing on the more sophisticated elements of the work such as perspective in creative writing, drawing and drama work. The suggestions below are offered here to illustrate how such an initial whole-class session can lead to work differentiated to suit individuals:

•   Draw a map of the forest showing where Dennis' cave is located.
•   Use a cassette recorder to tape the story, complete with sound effects.
•   Draw a picture of Dennis' bedroom. What toys does he have?
•   Write or improvise the dialogue in which the small boy tells his version of the events to his mother.

- Write or improvise a story for young monsters in which the monsters get the better of the humans.
- Pretend you are Dennis' mum. Write a letter to or improvise her telephone conversation with the people who write stories about humans, complaining that what they write is giving Dennis nightmares.
- Write or improvise a scene to show what happens to someone else who gets lost in the forest and meets Dennis, assuming that Dennis *or* the lost person had been advised by the group.

The Monster Bed is a delightful story in its own right. The subversion of established beliefs is made clear through the use of language and illustration. This drama did not add anything that was not available in the story, though it helped the pupils to gain a perspective on what it was about and provided the opportunity of playing around in the boundaries of the narrative. Christine Warner (1997: 41), discussing means of recognising children's engagement in drama, quotes one 11-year-old as saying: 'When we are in drama, it is like walking in the pages of a book.' In this session that is precisely what the children did.

The Widow's Broom

In drama we try to communicate through the careful use of signs. Some of these are visual, some linguistic. When we go to the theatre, we expect everything we experience of the drama to have a purpose. An individual item on the set, such as a chair, may not in itself mean much. But if it is a particular type of chair, a throne for example or a very ornate antique chair, it might indicate something about the place in which the play is set or the type of person who will sit in it. As we watch the play our expectations will be reinforced or adjusted. Gradually, as the context builds, we will become clearer about the purpose of these signs and we will begin to find more meaning in the play.

To adopt the taxonomy of the philosopher C. S. Peirce (1955), signs which mean what they are may be called 'icons'. The figure of a person running from a fire on a fire exit sign is iconic in that it depicts nothing other than a person running from a fire. In the same way, the icon of a printer on a computer screen means 'printer', although, as with any taxonomy, this may be a simplification. Is it really true that a rose is a rose is a rose? Is it not more accurate to recognise that we interpret everything in terms of both personal experience and cultural convention? Thus, the fire exit sign may be baffling to someone who has never seen a fire, and a rose will have vastly different meanings for someone who is an incurable romantic and someone who is a keen gardener.

Signs which seem to point beyond themselves to something else are called 'indexes'. Smoke is an index of fire, a fire exit sign is an index of the exit to be used in the event of a fire. Thus, an arrow on a sign is clearly an index of direction; it does not just mean 'Here is an arrow'! Whereas smoke will be seen as a universal index of fire, it is clear that some indexes acquire their value in specific cultural contexts, that is, we *learn* that they are indexes. Thus it is that a 'besom' in our culture is likely to be recognised as more than just a type of broom: it is an index, a visual metonym if you like, of a witch.

Some signs take on a special meaning. All art may be considered to involve the deliberate making of *symbols*, that is, signs that mean something beyond themselves Thus, the ritualised burning of the broom in this story by Chris Van Allsburg might be said to symbolise the witch herself but *also* the intolerance, prejudice and brutality of the men in the tale. A powerful symbol is likely to stand for more than just one other thing: it will have wide-ranging cultural and individual resonance. A powerful symbol will mean so much that the symbol itself will be the most economical way of expressing all of that meaning. In this way, art may be said to be 'meaning embodied', that is, the potential meanings cannot be adequately separated away from the work itself. Margaret Meek (1988: 10) points out that while beginning readers have the capacity to recognise the symbolic interactions at work in the process of reading stories, teachers all too frequently miss the opportunity to help pupils enquire into them and understand them for what they are. What teachers might usefully do, and drama is an effective way of doing it, is to find structures which allow children to locate and play with their own interpretations of the symbolic. If literary competence does involve more than simply recognizing words on a page, it must surely involve the ability to recognise the symbolic.

In order to reveal the symbolic potential of texts in classroom drama, the teacher must be careful in her use of *focus* and *frame*. What the children see and hear needs to be clear and uncluttered. This may mean, for example, isolating things the teacher wants the children to talk about in a certain space in the same way that children might investigate mini-beasts by putting them under a magnifier. It also suggests that the tasks set in the drama must be clearly described.

All stories may be considered in terms of three questions:

1   What characters are involved?
2   What happens in the narrative?
3   What themes does the story present to the reader?

Some stories should be considered in terms of context also: Where/when was it set?

A liberating aspect of some stories is that they are set in a 'Once-upon-a-time' land, and with such stories there is no need to be specific about all of their logistical details as the possibility of magic happening is acceptable. In the best stories, however, there is always a price to pay for magic. Consider the dilemma of the maiden in *Rumpelstiltskin*, for example, and match this against the cliché that many children use to get out of the most tense moment in their own storywriting – the discovery that it was in fact all a dream! Brian Woolland (1993) has pointed out that clearly stating the limitations of magic makes for better drama. The whole concept of dramatic tension in plays or in novels is popularly expressed as being 'between the Devil and the deep blue sea'. In Chris Van Allsburg's story, the broom is clearly a very mixed blessing for the widow; in the end it is not magic that saves her but her own cunning in turning people's prejudices against themselves.

The sessions

Described below is the sequence followed in two forty-minute drama sessions with 7–8-year-olds at Whitelands Park Primary School in Thatcham, Berkshire, along with some commentary arising from a reflection on this work. The objectives were to explore how the story could be seen as a parable about prejudice, and to give the pupils the opportunity of adopting and sustaining dramatic roles. Another objective was to help the children see how the visual images in the book carry meaning and how using this visual literacy could enrich the pupils' own attempts at drama.

1   A besom, a shawl and a stick were laid out on the floor and the children were asked to sit around them. They were told the drama was going to feature these three objects but that first they needed to discover what sort of a drama it would be just by looking at them. They passed around and handled each item in turn, commenting on anything they noticed about them. The deictical value of these objects was very strong, and the children quickly concluded that the story would involve an old woman, an old man and possibly a witch. They suggested that the people were poor and had to work hard (the broom signified work, the shawl feeling cold/poverty and the stick a rural setting). These signals pointed to a 'once-upon-a-time' framework. In picture-books, as in drama, the selection of visual images which convey so much so economically is as important as is the selection of words in a poem. Indeed, Susanne Langer (1953) has described drama as 'an enacted poem'.

2   After finding a space for themselves, the children were asked to imagine a village in a fairy story and to walk around the room miming going to different places in the village. In this way the children were invited to ensure that there was a distance between the story to be created and their own present realities.

    They were asked to imagine watching somebody at work, then to freeze in a position that suggested that work. These still images were animated through movement and sound.

The children had a clear reference point in this work. Like all children (in Britain at least) they knew a lot about 'once-upon-a-time land', and so had no trouble visualising what people did there. It was not the purpose of this drama to challenge such stereotypes, though the safety offered by stereotypes would be questioned as the session developed.

3   In pairs, the children found out about each other's job. Crucially, the teacher also questioned the pupils at this point. Thoughts about the life of the villagers were then gathered.

Their jobs were to become 'hooks' for the characters; that is, no matter what else happened in the drama, it would always be possible to refer back to their chosen jobs. Quite a lot of context had been built so far: the drama had a setting and lots of characters. It now needed interaction and narrative focus. Throughout, but especially when collecting ideas about the work, the teacher should look for ways to heighten the children's response by asking leading questions, listening and reacting to the answers and rephrasing them so that the ensuing submission grows in stature and usefulness:

TEACHER: What is your job?
CHILD: A baker.
TEACHER: A baker? Are there many bakers in this town?
CHILD: Only me.
TEACHER: Just you? You must be very busy. Do you have a family to help? . . .

4   The children were asked to imagine a marketday in the village; it was suggested that perhaps they wanted to buy or sell some things, but if nothing else they would still have their special jobs to do. They were informed that a character whom they knew would come to the marketplace, and that after her appearance they would be asked their opinion of her. The market was set up and the teacher entered in role as a rather helpful and kindly old woman. After a few minutes the improvisation was halted, and the children said what they thought of this character.

The teacher played the woman as a stereotype: she appeared harmless and even a little helpless. It was important to make her an object of some sympathy in order to create a dilemma later. The snatches of dialogue also gave the teacher the chance to reinforce the children's chosen roles.

5   The children were given the chance to talk to the woman and, through hot-seating, they discovered a little more about her life. Some children were also invited to take the hot-seat in role as the woman. The character was extended by inviting the class, in role as villagers,

to ask her questions so giving her an attitude to which she could respond.

6   The teacher narrated how, the following week, in the same village, just as people were going about their business in the marketplace, the woman arrived again but this time things were a little different. Having set the scene, the teacher entered in role again and solicited help with a number of carts which seemed to be weighed down with goods. She did not wish to sell the goods but either gave them away or accepted ridiculous offers for them, for example a bunch of flowers for a stack of logs. The children were asked to comment on what had happened, and focused immediately on the question of where all the stuff had come from.

(One might also have asked the pupils to think of something they might say to the woman, then listen to the responses in turn as they are spoken aloud. The woman was always signified by the shawl and these last comments could have been addressed to the shawl as it hung over a chair.)

All of the activities in this session were being developed in parallel to the actual text of which the children had, at this point, no knowledge. The intention was to give the children's characters an attitude towards the woman while raising a genuine mystery in their minds.

7   The second session opened with a recap on the story thus far. The children were asked to play out the scene in which they were returning home from the market carrying the items of food and the logs they had received from the widow. The teacher, in role now as a man with a stick, asked them individually where they had got the stuff. He became increasingly agitated as he spoke to more people. It was clear from his manner that he was someone who expected to be respected. After the scene the children were asked to talk about who they thought he was and what he was like. It was agreed that while he had no real power in the village, he was someone of whom people were a little frightened. Here again the gender stereotype was deliberate. The teacher's concern was to get the children to consider what they should do about the widow's strange new ability to produce food and firewood. A meeting would be the best forum for this but as the children had not suggested that the old man was the mayor or had some official status narration was employed to indicate that a meeting was being held later in the day. That evening, the villagers gathered on the green to share the things they had made with the widow's produce. Into this scenario entered the old man to warn them of the evil they were encouraging. From here it was necessary to go along with the way the children developed the scene. Given that both protagonist and antagonist were now established, the children themselves could be invited to play those roles.

Two options were seen as viable at this juncture:

- either the pupils went against the widow and destroyed the broom (in which case how would they help her out in the future; or, if they punished her, how would they justify that?);
- or, the villagers agreed to let woman keep the broom and use it to provide them with food and logs (in which case what would happen when the people from the next village found out?).

A major intention in the drama was to encourage the children to make their own decisions and then get them to see the consequences of those decisions.

8   In role as the old man, the teacher introduced the rumour that the widow had a magic broom. The children decided to break into the widow's cottage and demand to see it. While in the cottage one girl found a scrap of paper (this was her invention) which revealed how the broom might be destroyed. ('First burn it, then pour water over its embers', she pretended to read.) Another girl, spontaneously donning the mantle of the widow, shooed the villagers from the cottage and successfully made them feel guilty for bursting in. In role as the old man, the teacher pressed the villagers into deciding what to do about the 'wicked' broom. By this time they were turning against the old man, seeing him as just a jealous and vindictive old troublemaker. They decided to go and apologise to the widow, but also to suggest that the broom represented a threat – her use of it to produce things to give away had brought trouble to the village, though they realised that this had not been her intention. That being the case, they suggested that the broom be destroyed. The widow agreed, and the children ritualistically destroyed the broom.

This was a rounded conclusion to the drama session, and it was at this point that the book was read and the pictures shown to the class. They attended closely to the story's details, seeming at each turn of the page to be weighing up the similarities and differences between what they now heard and saw and what they had had a hand in creating. The dramatic structure had worked at the level of myth in that the 'problem' was solved according to the class's existing value system. Showing them the book afterwards, however, offered a very different experience. The depictions of the vulnerable, not to say sensuous, young witch, the simple yet curiously endearing broom and the pinched and miserable looking villagers, initially silenced the children. My interpretation of their reaction is that they had suddenly seen themselves as having re-enacted the myth; a process which in itself had revealed the parable. Subsequent discussion about the story illustrated their recognition that the way they had behaved had been as misinformed and ill-judged as were the reactions of the villagers in the story book.

Conclusion

I started this chapter by making the somewhat obvious claim that there is nothing wrong with simply looking at books as they are. As Steve Cockett has argued, two common purposes of story are to:

> remind ourselves of what we already know, to confirm our view that the world is, essentially, the place we thought it was, [and] to challenge our perceptions and beliefs by putting them to the test.
>
> (1997: 7)

By using drama in conjunction with the story as it is told in a book teachers may be able to effectively explore the parabolic elements of the story by embodying the dramatic tension and thus making the problem which drives the narrative more concrete and more immediate. In this way, children may justifiably feel that they not only 'know' the problem but can feel comfortable with its existence given that they have had a hand in creating the hypothesis it presents.

On the face of it, the programme prescribed for the Literacy Hour is somewhat mechanistic. However, a closer inspection of the programme reveals that drama is most certainly recognised as playing a part in the development of literary competence. Detractors may criticise the conception of the Literacy Hour as signalling a return 'under the "back to basics" banner ... to discredited "child-centred" methods that depend on pupils discovering things for themselves' (*Daily Telegraph*, 14 January 1998). The argument forwarded in this chapter is that the very process of reading words and images *entails* pupils 'discovering things for themselves'. The joy of reading, it seems to me, is precisely this sense of discovery for oneself. That is the 'basic' which needs to be realised. For their part, teachers have an important role in encouraging such a sense of discovery in children. I believe that drama can be an effective method of doing just that, and hope that the practical examples given above help to demonstrate this.

Not every storybook, however, immediately lends itself to a dramatising approach, and applying dramatic methods too frequently would perhaps limit the pupils' awareness that texts may be interpreted in different ways and through different modes. It would also become as tiresome as 'plodding through' the text.

Choosing the picture-books which lend themselves to drama is itself no simple matter, but the guidelines below may help you spot the potential of those that do:

- Look for books that tell stories in which there seem to be 'gaps' in the action, that is, where something must have happened which is not clearly told. For example, in Nigel Gray's *I'll Take You to Mrs Cole* (1985) a small boy is threatened by his mother with a neighbour who she has mythologised into an ogre. At the end of the book the mother's attitude towards Mrs Cole has changed, but we are not told exactly how this change has come about. Through drama children may explore the possibilities.

- Look for stories which suggest other stories. In Margaret Mahy's *The Man Whose Mother Was a Pirate* (1987), Mr Fat receives a letter from his ex-employee, the Little Man and at the end invites him to run away and join him as a pirate. What adventures would the Little Man have had that would make him send such a letter? Does Mr Fat go? If so, what happens?

- Stories which show the different attitudes of people seem to me to have more potential than those which focus on narrating events. *The Monster Bed*, as we have seen, is suitable for use with young children because it gives a clear illustration of how ignorance, especially when reinforced by adults, can lead to unnecessary fear, and perhaps also to discomfort when the truth is discovered. Older children might explore the roots of similar prejudices through *The Widow's Broom* which touches on, but never fully explores, prejudices against anything new and strange, as well as prejudices about single women.

A final note: the sessions described above used picture-books in the context of the primary school, but applying drama methods to the study of novels in the secondary school can be equally effective, and would serve the same purpose. Furthermore, I do not believe that there is a sound rationale for using picture-books only with children of primary-school age. Drawing older pupils' attention to the power of visual images is equally vital if they are to appreciate the myriad visual images with which they are daily bombarded and use this understanding to make richer dramas of their own. The strength of any good story is that it can engage people over a broad age range, and picture-books such as *I'll Take You to Mrs Cole* and *The Widow's Broom* may stimulate work of considerable aesthetic and moral value in the upper years of the secondary school.

References

Bettelheim, B. (1976) *The Uses of Enchantment*, London: Penguin.
Carter, A. (1982) *Sleeping Beauty and Other Favourite Fairy Tales*, London: Gollancz.
Cockett, S. (1997) 'Drama, myth and parable: problem-solving and problem knowing', *Research in Drama Education*, Vol. 2, No. 1.
Fine, A. (1989) *Goggle-Eyes*, London: Puffin.
Goodwyn, A. (1994) *English and Ability*, Milton Keynes: Open University Press.
Gray, N. (1985) *I'll Take You To Mrs Cole*, London: Macmillan.

Langer, S. (1953) *Feeling and Form*, London: Routledge & Kegan Paul.

Mahy, M. (1987) *The Man Whose Mother Was a Pirate*, London: Picture Puffins.

Meek, M. (1988) *How Texts Teach What Readers Learn*, Stroud: Thimble Press.

National Literacy and Numeracy Project (1997) *Framework for Teaching* (Draft), London: DfEE.

Peirce, C. S. (1955) *Philosophical Writings*, ed. J. Buchler, New York: Dover.

Van Allsburg, C. (1992) *The Widow's Broom*, London: Anderson Press.

Warner, C. (1997) 'The edging in of engagement: exploring the nature of engagement in drama', *Research in Drama Education*, Vol. 2, No. 1.

Willis, J. (1986) *The Monster Bed*, London: Arrow Books.

Woolland, B. (1993) *The Teaching of Drama in the Primary School*, London: Longman.

Zipes, J. (1976) *Breaking the Magic Spell*, London: Heinemann.

—— (1994) *Fairy Tale as Myth, Myth as Fairy Tale*, Lexington, KY: University Press of Kentucky.

Chapter 6

Drawing lessons from Anthony Browne

Mary Purdon

The children in my class (years 1 and 2 mixed) were already avid readers of picture-books, familiar with the selection of authors and illustrators available in the classroom, such as Mitsumasa Anno, David McKee, Jill Murphy, Shirley Hughes, the Ahlbergs, John Burningham, Anthony Browne, Satoshi Kitamura and Hiawyn Oram, Jeannie Baker, etc. My starting-point for the project which is described in this chapter was to tap into their enjoyment of this genre and to help them look more critically at picture-books: not as art objects, but as texts where words and pictures work together. I also wanted my young readers to be able to talk about their response to picture-books as a whole, and to give them tools which they could use to develop that response. I decided to focus on books written and illustrated by Anthony Browne, as his work was already popular with my class and he is one of the finest illustrators of children's books today. The main elements I chose to concentrate on were: *intertextuality* – references to other texts and artists; *colour symbolism*; and *layout*, or what Jane Doonan refers to as 'objects in space' – 'the weight given to the object by its siting on the page' (Doonan 1993).

I wanted to explore ways of probing what children made of the metaphors they read, and to see how they responded to the visual references Anthony Browne makes. His books include references to works by a wide range of well-known artists, both painters and film-makers, and I was delighted when he published *Willy the Dreamer* (1997), towards the end of our project, with its direct references to many of his favourite artists and characteristic rich visual intertextuality.

In *Looking at Pictures in Picture Books* (1993), Jane Doonan says that '[P]upils bring with them more implicit knowledge than they know what to do with', and I wanted to help my pupils to find some ways of exploring and sharing that knowledge. In the words of Helen Bromley (1996): 'The teacher's job is to enable children to make their intertextual knowledge explicit.' As my class of 5- and 6-year-olds pored over Anthony Browne's illustrations (having been trained by *The Jolly Postman*, with a lens), looking for his hidden pictures, I would wonder whether they understood some of the less obvious visual references and jokes and, if they did, what such understanding brought to their reading of the book.

Intertextuality

I invited Toni Russell, an art teacher, to introduce the notion of surrealism to my class. She explained that we understand what we see in relationship to what is around it, and that surrealists wanted to put the 'play' back into art work, and to make people think about *why* things are the way they are. She illustrated difficult concepts with examples and, despite the complexity of the subject, the children were soon very involved. We then went on to look carefully at Magritte's *The Fall*, and some of the children drew versions of it to help them understand how Magritte worked. They pored over collections of Magritte's paintings and sculptures, fascinated by even the a very small black-and-white reproduction that demonstrated the development of his ideas. Finally, I showed them Anthony Browne's *Through the Magic Mirror*, and was rewarded by a chorus of 'Look, it's Magritte!', when they saw the cover, and huge excitement about the falling choirboys. The reference to Magritte's *Golconde* was instantly recognised: the painting had been a favourite of the class, and many children had made their own version of it (see Figure 6.1).

They wanted to go back over the pictures in our books on Magritte to confirm similarities and differences, and to discuss them with their friends.

I subsequently asked the children why they thought Anthony Browne used such clear references to another artist.

LEON: I know, I know, it reminds me of when, in there [points to Magritte book] when those men were flying, coming down, it was like they were falling from air.

MP: Why do you think Anthony Browne's done this then?

LEON: To make you think of that one. He's done different people 'cos he didn't want to copy.

MP: How is it different from Magritte's one?

LEON: They're just standing there with the mouths like this [demonstrates], but Anthony Browne's got more colour and different... [demonstrates arm movements].

Leon was clear that Anthony Browne wants his readers to recognise the reference to Magritte and was able to notice and explain the ways in which the picture had been adapted, fully accepting that the author would not want to be seen as 'copying' someone else's work!

I told the children that *Through the Magic Mirror* was the first book that Anthony Browne had published, and read them the passage from 'Making

Figure 6.1 Magritte's work appealed to Tom's sense of humour, and his creative work began to make direct references to pictures he had studied.

picture books' (Browne 1994: 179) where he describes the genesis of that text, and how he has since developed the relationship between text and pictures in his work: 'when I put jokes or details of surrealistic stuff in the background I try to make it have a point, I try to give it relevance in the story'. I also read them parts of Browne's description of the symbolism used in his illustrations for *Hansel and Gretel* (1981), after they had had the chance to explore the book for themselves, and many of the children were delighted to find that the recurrent prison bars and witch's hats they had noticed for themselves had been included to stress, on the one hand, the powerlessness and loss of freedom which poverty imposes on people, and, on the other, the possible relationship between the stepmother and the witch. As Morag Styles points out in 'Inside *The Tunnel*' (1996), Anthony Browne's texts excite children by their 'humour and profundity'. She observed two boys who were 'deeply engaged in unravelling the many perplexing motifs in Browne's work: unworried by surrealist imagery, visual puns or enigmatic representation, they scrutinized the text with great determination to find every possible incongruity'. One of the pleasures of working with children is their enthusiasm for sharing their discoveries about the texts they are reading: new insights were spread rapidly around the class, and an unfamiliar book or a different edition was seized upon with delight.

We moved on to look at Browne's *Changes*, which follows the story of a boy who has been told that things were going to change. This is one of the most surreal of Browne's books, and there are numerous visual references throughout the story to the most important change of all, which is revealed at the end of the book: the birth of the new baby. There we found not only Magritte, in the slipper changing into a bird and the man's leg on the washbasin, but a copy of Van Gogh's famous bedroom scene. Our subsequent study of Van Gogh's paintings included exploring his swirling, bold brush strokes, and the rich colours of his landscapes (see Figure 6.2). Haitham, who had recently arrived in the class, having come from Egypt, and was only just beginning to speak English, was very excited to find that the same patterns of brush strokes used by Van Gogh were on the wall of the house in Anthony Browne's illustration, and went back to the original to check that he was right. He then spent nearly a whole day painting his own version of the bedroom, which was recognisably Van Gogh's until he decided to cover it with black paint! This was a major breakthrough for him, as he had had no previous experience of painting or drawing at school and was unfamiliar with a culture of picture-books.

The children became expert detectives, and often wanted to know whether a picture on a wall was 'a real one'. I had shown them the part of 'Making picture books', in which Anthony Browne describes the final illustrated scene for *Hansel and Gretel*, with the new shoot growing optimistically in the plant pot and a painting by Arnold Bocklin on the wall (to which we were unable to find any reference). Browne wrote:

> I often use paintings on the wall to try to tell another aspect of the story – I hope this isn't seen as 'winking over the child's shoulder' – sharing a joke or some reference with the adult. I think as long as the images work in the context of the story, it's just another layer.
>
> (Browne 1994: 185)

We looked also at the Gainsborough hung over the Piggots' mantelpiece in *Piggybook*, in which Browne has left a space where, in the original, the wife would be, and talked about pictures with which the children were familiar. The children were surprisingly sophisticated in their awareness of cultural icons, especially cinematic icons. I had not expected them to know that the gorilla standing on the air vent on the way to the pool in *Willy the Champ* was Marilyn Monroe, but it was obviously a familiar image to several children. They also recognised King Kong in *Gorilla*, so we moved on to Anthony Browne's own version of *King Kong*. I thought it might be too difficult for such young children, but it struck a chord with one group of boys, both because of the dinosaurs and because of the style. 'Like Dick

Figure 6.2 Marena liked the colours and shapes in Van Gogh's paintings and spent a long time over her version of Van Gogh's Cypresses.

Tracy', Leigh said, immediately identifying the genre of old American movies. Most of this group had seen the film *King Kong*, which they thought very sad, identifying with the great ape under attack rather than the heroine.

Helen Bromley (1996) discusses the use of 'icons' by children in the way they associate certain figures or imagery with particular authors. Such use is to be encouraged, she says, as part of the ability to develop and test hypotheses about writers and texts. She quotes Annabel Thomas's *Illustrated Dictionary of Narrative Painting* (1994) on the important role played by 'circumstantial details' in supporting the story they illustrate, and suggests that it is this detail which 'draws the children back to the picture books again and again'. Children feel at home with the idea that illustrators have favourite themes, just as they themselves have: in the same way as Edward always draws trains, and the whole class can recognise Danielle's style of people, so Shirley Hughes draws plump toddlers with curly hair, and Anthony Browne likes monkeys and gorillas. The psychologist Victor Lowenfield (1939), in his analysis of creative development, called these themes 'schema', and found that such representations are closely bound up with the individual self. The melancholy of the caged apes in several of Browne's books struck a chord with many children. Charlie, who spent hours poring over *Zoo* and *Gorilla*, later wrote this poem:

Life in a cage
A monkey living in its cage,
Waiting to be let out.
Sitting on its tyre,
Waiting and waiting.
I went to the zoo and saw the monkey.
I was weeping.
People were throwing stones.
Then I knew what he was thinking.
He wanted to be in the jungle
With his other monkey friends,
And his family miss him.

Colour symbolism

Earlier in the term we had spent a lot of time talking about colours and the moods they might induce or reflect. Using a range of percussion instruments, the children composed and then danced to music that reflected their feelings about a particular colour. We also listened to jazz, reggae, harp and waltz music and then painted pictures with the colours each piece inspired, which provided a useful insight into the very different ways in which people can react to the same thing! The children needed little prompting to talk about the way in which Anthony Browne uses colours in *Hansel and Gretel*:

sepia-toned, dark, shadowy pictures where the children are miserable, lost or frightened, and a rainbow over blue sky when they escape from the witch, with the door open to bright light as they reach home and their father's arms. The children noticed that the stepmother wore bright colours, 'pretending to be nice', like the witch's tempting cherry-cake trap.

Layout

In order to discuss the pictures in the class books, we needed to collect the appropriate technical terms. These were put on cards and written up in the book corner, and the children were quick to pick up and use words like 'text', 'frontispiece' and 'endpaper'. We looked at the endpapers in *The Tunnel*, where Anthony Browne elegantly symbolises the whole story of the relationship between the brother and sister: the boy's ball and the girl's book, separated on contrasting pages at the beginning, and lying companionably together at the end. The children became very keen to explore the endpapers, earnestly discussing whether they were exact copies or reflections of the opposite end, and why a pattern or picture had been chosen. Kita's response was typical looking at *Willy and Hugh*: 'Look, there are two bananas on this endpaper, 'cos now there's him *and* his friend.' This led to a frantic search for other Willy books to check their endpapers, confirming the initial idea (there is only one banana in the endpaper for *Willy the Wimp*), but also leading to the discovery that paperback versions often have no endpapers. (I was disappointed to find that several of the library editions had covered up the endpapers.) The children's experience had led them to expect to find significance in the details of the books they studied. They already knew about copyright, carefully drawing little © marks on their own books and pictures, and now they were able to compare different editions of the same story, noticing publishers' symbols and even different fonts.

We discussed frames and looked also at ways in which the illustrators separated pictures and text on a page. The children noticed that the pictures in *The Night Shimmy* are set within heavy black frames with the text printed in white on black paper, reflecting Eric's gloomy situation, alone and friendless, until he frees the kite and also himself, at which point the pictures fill the page and the facing pages are white and light. There was much turning of pages and discussion about what was happening, and the children were very interested when I found the technical term for this:

> **Bleed** A picture 'bleeds' if it extends to the trimmed edge of the paper. . . . The effect suggests a life going on beyond the confines of the page so that the beholder becomes more of a participant in than a spectator of the pictured events.
>
> (Doonan 1993: 81)

We discussed the placing on the page of the main character and the positioning of other objects. Every book in the Book Corner lent itself to this analysis, even if the pictures made no direct reference to other artists' work, and the children were able to discuss their own responses to different styles. I found them deliberating over the positioning of text and pictures when they made their own books, sometimes trying several ways and asking friends for their response.

The children were becoming critical readers who were very aware that authors made deliberate choices about colour and space, and that the illustrations are an intrinsic part of the story rather than an optional extra. They wanted to know the right words for parts of the book or pictures – I had to refer to Victor Watson (1996) myself to find out that the little pictures that Anthony Browne often uses on the title page were called 'vignettes' – and began to use them confidently in their discussions.

It was nearly a year after the lessons described that Anthony Browne published *Willy the Dreamer* (1997), and one parent triumphantly brought in a copy as a present for the class. It is one of Browne's finest texts, with the greatest number of intertextual references, both to his own books and to other artists, and it was seized on avidly. I watched to see what the children had remembered of our discussions about art and artists. There were delighted cries of recognition and the art books were retrieved from the library to check references. The children could not wait to show Toni, and ask her about the pictures in *Willy the Dreamer* that they did not recognise, utterly confident that they were references to 'real' paintings. She found the originals of some of the pictures for us, including one by de Chirico (shown in the illustration for Willy's dream about not being able to run). Toby stated: 'Willy can't run because he's got roots', but also made a connection with another text when he concluded that 'his toes are on the lines so it's bad luck'. A. A. Milne's poem may not have been in Anthony Browne's mind when he drew Willy, but Toby was sure that Willy's predicament was due to his stepping on the lines.

Danielle thought that Anthony Browne had used frames for the pictures of Willy's dreams because 'he doesn't want them to escape from the page', while Leon decided that it was 'an art gallery'. Maisie started the search for bananas by announcing: 'there's still bananas 'cos Willy eats bananas', and it was discovered that bananas were a recurrent theme in every picture and on the endpapers. Other intertextual references that the children quickly discovered were to Buster Nose, the bully who first appears in *Willy the Wimp* ('Look, he's running out of the frame'), and the Fair Isle pattern on Willy's jumper, which even appears on a banana. The book provoked week after week of discussion, and I had to get another copy and draw up a rota for taking it home. I expected the children to recognise the Tenniel illustrations for *Alice in Wonderland* in Willy's dream of being a famous writer, but was surprised that so many of them also knew the references in his dream about fierce monsters, until Oliver explained: 'He's the beast – that's in *The Pagemaster* – Dr Jekyll and Mr Hyde, like *Julia Jekyll and Harriet Hyde* on television. Beauty and the Beast is another, it's both of the same really.' These children feel confident with a wide range of visual texts, moving freely between traditional fiction, video and television, and spotting references that I had not noticed, for example in the dream about super heroes:

OLIVER: Look, Superman and Batman!
JESS: Playing with the dolls' house, it's *Toy Story* 'cos of the wallpaper.
OLIVER: It's Buzz Lightyear, they're all toys.

The recognition of such minor details as the wallpaper in the background of a popular cartoon film shows the level of involvement with both texts: the children are interested and highly perceptive – they *expect* to find meaning in every part of a Browne illustration.

The children's detective-work enabled them to recognise many direct references to Magritte's paintings, but they had not yet come across Salvador Dali. The picture of Willy's dream of being in a strange landscape provoked strong reactions:

MAISIE: I don't like this one, it's a bit, like, ghosty and people being murdered.
LEON: Like a nightmare, everything's really quiet.
MAISIE: This makes me feel like a hot desert, like you've run out of water.
DANIELLE: It's funny, strange. He looks confused.
TOBY: He's feeling scared, a little bit lonely.

I then showed them some paintings by Salvador Dali, and they spent hours looking for references that Anthony Browne had used, finding the flaming giraffes, drooping landscapes and sinister drawers, and then turning back to Magritte to check that he too had painted flaming objects in his *Ladder of Fire*. Everyone had something to contribute, a new observation or suggestion to make, and there was a constant rereading of other Anthony Browne books to reaffirm memories of references. Toby thought that it would be useful if Anthony Browne had included a 'list of pictures at the back so you can check', which showed his familiarity with reference books. Someone noticed that the figure of Willy in the last picture is 'melting in' to the chair, his shoes empty, and there was a lot of turning back and forth to compare this with the first picture. In this last scene, Anthony Browne is not winking over the child's shoulder, but directly at the young reader, with an invitation to enjoy the jokes. Everyone who reads the book is a complicit reader who can take the text at whatever level suits them, and it is this sharing of allusions that makes Anthony Browne's books so popular with children of all ages.

Developing the children's critical awareness and providing them with the technical terms they need in order to be precise about their observations is an essential part of enabling them to become readers. In *Looking at Pictures in Picture Books* (1993), Jane Doonan discusses the idea that the experience of engaging with a picture-book is one of 'play', where something personal is created from the ideas it provokes. She argues that abstract concepts have to be dealt with 'logically, intuitively and imaginatively', and that children need to be shown ways of doing this, 'to be given insights about ways of interpreting pictures in order to develop aesthetically: that they need knowledge if they are to move from an impression of pictures to an awareness of possible reasons for them' (ibid.: 7). She suggests that the 'crucial step' is when children begin to grasp ways in which pictures express ideas, moods, abstract notions and qualities, and that they can begin to explore beyond the literal representation once they have been shown 'how lines and shapes and colours are able to refer to ideas and feelings' (ibid.).

Although children often have an instinctive awareness of the significance of ideas and feelings expressed by illustrations, implicit understanding becomes explicit when they acquire a working vocabulary with which to think and communicate. Children often want to absorb a book without having to provide evidence of their understanding to adults, and that understanding is not easily explained. Jane Doonan uses the phrase 'loss in translation' to describe this disparity between the awareness of what is happening in the pictures and the ability to articulate that awareness. In 'The left-handed reader', Victor Watson raises another important issue in his fascinating description of Ann, a child who was absorbed by the pictorial text but seemed unwilling to decode the printed text in picture-books. When, eventually, Ann learned to read the words, Watson pointed out that it was at the expense of her 'ability to spin subtle narrative webs out of pictures' (Watson 1996: 161).

The guidance for teachers on the teaching of reading in the *National Literacy Strategy* (1998) makes no direct mention of reading pictures or using pictorial texts. It may, however, be implicit in some sections, for example where it states that children should be taught 'to predict what a given book might be about from a brief look at both front and back covers, including blurb, title, illustration; to discuss what it might tell in advance of reading and check if it does' (1998: 23), although that is included under non-fiction and again in referring to the ability 'to compare books by the same author: settings, characters, themes; to evaluate and form preferences, giving reasons' (ibid.: 30).

The emphasis throughout the *National Literacy Strategy* is explicitly upon the *written* text, yet awareness of the relationship between words and pictures in high-quality children's books will need to be developed by teachers, who are aware of the importance of intertextuality and multilayered meanings.

This is a vital part of text-level work, with children learning and using a wide range of technical terms to discuss the books they read. *The National Literacy Strategy* takes no account of the children's fascination with visual text, nor of their ability to understand references. If encouraged to see that an author has deliberately alluded to a picture in order to enrich the meaning of the text, then children will have no problems with the concept of literary allusion, or with meanings beyond the literal. They will appreciate that there can be individual responses to a text, and they will know that worthwhile texts repay reading over and over again, at all stages of life.

Jane Doonan's description of picture-books as art objects is true to the extent that the pictures are often works of art in themselves, but the books are far more than the sum of their individual pictures. The best books that we can give children are those which engage their emotions and respect their wide knowledge of, and intense curiosity about the complex multimedia world that they bring to reading. My class started their exploration with one author and the references he makes to art, culture, ideas and feelings. I have been surprised and impressed by the eagerness with which they have responded to the ideas we discussed. They are not perturbed by intertextuality, but seize upon it as a puzzle to solve, confident that they can make the connections, or that someone else in the class can. They are generous in accepting alternative suggestions, and are becoming sophisticated readers of colour, mood, meaning and image. They have become knowledgeable about artists and artistic conventions, and are interested in and open to new ideas about visual and written texts alike. They have developed critical skills (in both senses) for their future as readers.

References

Bromley, Helen (1996) 'Spying on picturebooks: exploring intertextuality with young children', in Victor Watson and Morag Styles (eds), *Talking Pictures: Pictorial Texts and Young Readers*, London: Hodder & Stoughton.

Browne, Anthony (1994) 'Making picture books', in M. Styles, E. Bearne and V. Watson (eds) *The Prose and the Passion*, London: Cassell.

DfEE (1998) *The National Literacy Strategy: Framework for Teaching*, London: HMSO.

Doonan, Jane (1993) *Looking at Pictures in Picture Books*, Stroud: Thimble Press.

Lowenfield, V. (1939) *The Nature of Creative Activity*, London: Routledge & Kegan Paul.

Styles, Morag (1996) 'Inside *The Tunnel*: a radical kind of reading – picture books, pupils and post-modernism', in Watson and Styles (eds).

Thomas, Annabel (1994) *The Illustrated Dictionary of Narrative Painting*, London: John Murray in association with the National Gallery.

Watson, Victor (1996) 'The left-handed reader; linear sentences and unmapped pictures', in Watson and Styles (eds).

Picture-books referred to in the text

Ahlberg, A. and Ahlberg, J. (1986) *The Jolly Postman*, London: Heinemann.

Browne, Anthony (1976) *Through the Magic Mirror*, London: Picture Puffin.

—— (1983) *Gorilla*, London: Julia MacRae Books.

—— (1984) *Willy the Wimp*, London: Julia MacRae Books.

—— (1985) *Willy the Champ*, London: Julia MacRae Books.

—— (1986) *Piggybook*, London: Julia MacRae Books.

—— (1989) *The Tunnel*, London: Julia MacRae Books.

—— (1990) *Changes*, London: Julia MacRae Books.

—— (1991) *Willy and Hugh*, London: Julia MacRae Books.

—— (1992) *Zoo*, London: Julia MacRae Books.

—— (1994) *King Kong*, London: Julia MacRae Books.

—— (1997) *Willy the Dreamer*, London: Walker Books.

Grimm, J. and Grimm, W. (1981) *Hansel and Gretel*, illust. Anthony Browne, London: Walker Books.

Strauss, Gwen and Browne, Anthony (1991) *The Night Shimmy*, London: Julia MacRae Books.

Chapter 7

Beyond the text

Metafictive picture-books and sophisticated readers

Kate Rabey

Fraser's short news bulletin

AN UNSOLVED MYSTERY
Yesterday two pigs got killed. It seems that a wolf killed them. Apparently the wolf is innocent, but we do not know what really happened. That's to be solved next time.

shows that this 6-year-old reader understands much about the ways in which texts are constructed, delivered and decoded. His item formed part of the class newspaper *'Pigsville News'*,[1] the creation of which was inspired by Scieszka and Smith's *The True Story of the Three Little Pigs* (1989). This chapter examines how *The True Story* and *The Stinky Cheese Man and Other Fairly Stupid Tales* (1992) by Scieszka and Smith rework traditional tales from a completely new angle and encourage children like Fraser to ask questions about texts. The anarchic energy of both texts invites powerful and inventive responses. This energy can be exploited and encouraged by the teacher to offer myriad possibilities which can be harnessed within the constraints of the Literacy Hour. In this chapter I attempt to unpick some of the metafictive devices which both author and illustrator employ in the hope this exploration will offer teachers an approach by which young readers may be encouraged and enabled to go 'beyond the text'.

Retellings – *The True Story of the Three Little Pigs*

The True Story is told from the wolf's point of view. He presents 'the facts' as if to correct earlier reports in which he has been misrepresented – 'nobody has ever heard my side of the story' – apparently telling the reader 'the truth' about the crime for which he has been convicted. Putting the reader–spectator in the position of judge and jury, Alexander Wolf's 'true story' is reminiscent of an Oprah Winfrey-style confessional, blaming his actions on factors outside his control: 'Hey, it's not my fault wolves eat cute little animals like bunnies and sheep and pigs. That's just the way they are. If cheeseburgers were cute, folk would probably think you were Big and Bad, too.'

The wolf's self-promoting title page screams out tabloid-like headings proclaiming 'This is the real story'. For the voice of the wolf, Scieszka borrows the style and speech pattern of a shady 1930s Raymond Chandler private investigator which adds to the informal and personal tone of his account – 'The rest, as they say, is history.' By including these intertextual references the authors are drawing readers' attention to the place of *The True Story* among other conventions and genres, which include both fiction and non-fiction. The child reader is being asked to make important distinctions between fantasy and reality, and the more experienced reader can enjoy the titillation of gangster movie nuances while reading a story for the young.

Questions raised by the written text are extended by Smith's pictures which contribute new metafictive dimensions through the introduction of freshly pasted newspaper headlines, first on the cover and again on the final few pages. The front page of *The Daily Wolf* is on the cover of the book, which prepares the reader for the wolf's story, 'as told to Jon Scieszka and Lane Smith'. Again, the sepia-tinted pages of the paper introduce more issues about the reliability of reported information, and the garbled text beneath the headlines seems to bear no relation to the story promised by the headlines and accompanying illustrations.

The same news is reported later in the book when the headlines of *The Daily Pig* scream 'BIG BAD WOLF!' Instead of the pig's trotter holding the paper as on the cover, *The Daily Pig* is clutched by a more human looking thumb. However, this hand could also belong to the wolf, further complicating the position of the narrator within the account. Although the newspaper text on this page is jumbled, there are a few more clues from which the reader can gain more information, such as the clever intertextual reference to another Big Bad Wolf in 'RED RIDING HOOD SETTLES DISPUTE OUT OF COURT'. The ambiguity of these collaged, irregular and incoherent tabloids introduce further questions about the stability of so-called truth and the authenticity of the wolf's account. As Jane Doonan asserts: 'Let this text teach.' Within this most amusing and enjoyable read, which forces the reader to sit up and engage, are important lessons for the learning. Every detail of text and image must be carefully considered for their legitimate inclusion as elements of the 'true' story, and the gaps in the composite account provided by images and narrative invite questions about truth and justice, and the position of the misrepresented outsider in the form of the wolf (Doonan 1991: 49).

The clever spread which accompanies the words 'THIS IS THE REAL STORY' asks some of the most crucial questions about the origins of reported stories. It deliberately draws the reader's attention to the status of any text as the product of imagination or invention. The letters which make up this powerful statement are taken from diverse sources. The 'I' is made from a curly pig's tail, the (second) 'E' represents a wolf's biting jaw and the 'O' is a pig snout. Conventional and respectable letter forms are also used, the (first) 'T' and (second) 'H' are printed in more-or-less traditional typeface, the (second) 'T' is torn from a newspaper.

Smith's choice of collage uses a technique favoured by surrealists (Ernst and Schwitters) and cubists (Braque and Picasso). The revolutionary work of these artists called into question the relationship between art and reality by including elements from the real world alongside the painted image. In *The True Story* the wolf makes his cake using photographed real eggs, milk and salt, and the portrait of his granny is hung behind him in a real frame. The child can find elements from their own concrete and apparently stable reality in these pasted fragments of photographed images which are juxtaposed with elements from the surreal and precarious world of fantasy.

Sendak, arguably the greatest American picture-book author and illustrator, describes the complex relationship between childhood and fantasy thus: 'Fantasy is all pervasive in a child's life. . . . Children do live in fantasy and reality in a way we no longer remember. They have a cool sense of the illogic, and they shift very easily from one sphere to another' (Sendak 1988).

The meanings and games found in these texts by the young audience for which they are written will perhaps always escape the adult reader. David Lewis describes it as a 'perpetual state of becoming. . . . What counts as a book and what counts as reading are, at this stage, not set in concrete' (Lewis 1991: 143). This indeterminacy is a central feature of much metafiction, and it adds to the exciting possibilities and reading experiences offered to the child by a dynamic and innovative text.

The retelling of this story is taken to excess, stretched to the very limits of credibility, and, in so doing, the narrative is being undermined. Authors delight in playing metafictive games with texts and pictures: 'In their artful and playful juxtaposition of image and word they often seek to draw attention to the fabric of the text itself' (Lewis 1992: 50); and they will make demands on the reader to think carefully about what is presented as fact as opposed to fiction. 'The broken rules and subverted conventions draw to the reader's attention the inner workings of the text and put up barriers against easy entry into the illusory world of realism' (ibid.: 62). *The True Story* parodies its status as text and fiction and draws the child's attention to the position of the storyteller within every account. These explorations can develop interpretive skills which help pupils to make sense of other texts, including television – the most pervasive storytelling medium of contemporary daily life.

Although the complexity of the text may present some problems for the inexperienced reader, the teacher can offer several 'ways in', as my colleague

Tiffany Astle's work with her class of 6-year-olds testifies. (It is interesting to note that Scieszka came up with the idea for the book after rewriting fairy tales with his second-grade class.) After reading *The True Story* and other traditional versions she engaged her class in a wide range of activities to deepen their understanding and enjoyment of the text. The class newspaper was written after several drama sessions in which members of the class had been invited to tell their own versions of the story. The teacher entered the classroom in the role of intrepid reporter, brandishing a home-made microphone and asking the children individually to give their accounts of what they had seen. In a later session the children became the television reporter, each taking a turn at broadcasting from inside a cardboard box with a cut-out screen. These sessions encouraged the children to think about the positions of both reporter and reported upon, as well as drawing on their own experience of watching and listening to television and radio news reports, revealing the wide range of styles and programmes with which the children were familiar. When 'in role', they were able to adopt the abrupt and dramatic 'news-speak' which was later recorded in *Pigsville News*, the class newspaper, as in the report by 6-year-old Amanda:

> *Two Dead Pigs!* Yesterday there were two pigs' houses blown down. One was sticks and one was straw and the wolf blew them down. It was in a wood. There was one more house and that was made of bricks. Now the pigs have eaten the wolf. Are we safe now?

Amanda's news flash shows that she has thought about how a story is constructed – by setting the scene and including only the bare facts. Her last sentence reveals a deeper understanding of the audience, bringing them into the violent string of events and questioning their personal safety, a twist reminiscent of sensationalised headline stories which play upon the darkest fears of their audience. As well as acting as a source of ideas for writing, *The True Story* could provide a discussion point about issues of authenticity and trust, and could be extended to a debate about the role and moral responsibility of the story-teller, perhaps in the context of our own controversial media and *paparazzi*.

Multilayered texts and readers in *The Stinky Cheese Man*

The Stinky Cheese Man and Other Fairly Stupid Tales also retells familiar fairy tales from a new perspective, and in so doing creates an exciting and challenging dialogue between reader and text. It is hard to see who is actually in control of the story, as Jack in his role as the narrator is continually usurped and upstaged by his lively cast of characters. The narrative is fractured and slips from one side to another, extending the possibilities of the text. The the title dominates the cover, its bold upper-case letters giving the reader a taste of the anarchic world which lurks within. With the Stinky Cheese Man taking the unlikely role of cover girl, we are introduced to some of the main characters along the spine of the book's cover. On the back cover we meet the bossy Little Red Hen, who demands in large red bold type: 'What is this doing here? This is ugly! Who is this ISBN guy?' Immediately subversive and aggressive, she here begins the process of questioning and parody which dominates the book. Readers are ordered to engage with the text even before they get to the first page.

Once inside the book the reader is introduced to the puckish Jack who sets up the dialogue by taking the roles of both narrator and chorus, chastising the Little Red Hen for her untimely interruption: 'Now why don't you just disappear for a few pages. I'll call you when I need you.' he plays a multiplicity of roles: he has a cameo part in the story of Jack and Jill, which is eclipsed by the dedication page; and in the story of Chicken Licken he flies into the page on a toy aeroplane. He features again in the window behind Cinderumpelstiltskin, as well as having a whole story to himself – which he uses to his benefit by tricking the giant into falling asleep. The reader has entered a story where the characters themselves are taking control, redirecting both the narrative and the way in which it is told.

This process of interruption is an important metafictive device, and it continues throughout the book as the characters fight one another for the reader's attention. Characters burst out of the pages of their own stories and find their ways into others, invading both pictures and text. Even the endpapers refuse to be pinned down. The wavy pastel colours create an optical illusion which gives the impression that they, too, are moving. The story of Chicken Licken starts too early and the characters are squashed by the Table of Contents as a punishment. In Little Red Running Shorts the Wolf and the main character have an argument with Jack and walk out of both the story and the illustration itself, leaving behind them their blank white silhouettes and an empty page.

The Stinky Cheese Man is an exhausting read. It bombards the reader with a multiplicity of perspectives and voices which can be difficult to separate one from the other. The perpetual dialogue between reader and text forces the reader to engage and to question. The book's complexity and aggressive energy seem to exert a strange power. Like a mischievous school-child, it refuses to obey the rules. (This is perhaps where the voice of the child lies throughout both this text and *The True Story*.) The indeterminacy of the text and pictures make the book at times an intensely frustrating one for an adult to read. While studying this ever-moving and energetic text, I found meanings which had earlier eluded me suddenly imposing themselves and discoveries being made. The layers of voices open possibilities for exciting retellings with older children. The narrative often appears as spoken text, and characters take centre stage for their own individual performance. A class study of the book might involve further retellings or even culminate in drama work where pupils are given the opportunity to experiment with different roles, retellings and voices.

Intertextuality

By cross-referencing traditional stories with contemporary media such as television and newspapers, Scieszka and Smith draw on the reader's existing knowledge of story and fairy tale, and they make a wide range of references to other texts. This enables the young reader to find elements of the familiar and provides anchors within their own experience. This borrowing from other sources is stretched to the ridiculous in *The Stinky Cheese Man*. In Giant Story the Giant cuts up an ancient leather-bound volume of fairy tales to paste together his own version, re-using familiar elements of the texts. Giant Story challenges convention by reversing the formulas used for the beginning and ending of fairy tales.

These intertextual references are added to by the collaged picture which accompanies the text and seems also to have been constructed by the giant, as his large fleshy fingers hold the side of the page. In this cubist collage there are more elements of familiar stories and tales which pay homage to the variety of sources from which the material for *The Stinky Cheese Man* was gathered. The child can find an old chapbook picture of Aesop, Aladdin's magic lamp, a golden slipper, a bitten-into poisoned apple, a magic harp, the Gingerbread Man, a fairy tale castle, a golden egg, two blind mice, the Tin Man, a blackbird baked in a pie, and many others. These intertextual references invite the reader to engage in a game of I-Spy which draws on their past knowledge of story and rhyme, and encourages an interaction with the words and pictures on the page. These collages add richness to the multi-layered text.

The double-spread page of Giant Story alone contains enough raw material for weeks' worth of Literacy Hour reading and writing. Pupils can be engaged as a team of detectives, hunting out the sources of these borrowed details. Or they can be encouraged to act as literary vandals, rebuilding their own stories and verses by pillaging extracts from others. At sentence level the layered narratives in *The Stinky Cheese Man* could offer a meaningful context for the study of grammar and punctuation, introducing as it does a confusing and diverse range of games with syntax and construction. A study of the whole book at text level might involve a complex unwrapping of the many layers of narrative and a careful mapping of intertextual links.

Throughout *The Stinky Cheese Man* these games at text and sentence levels are extended by the author's wordplay and meaning games, and by the way in which the typography is twisted and manipulated as part of the story. In the story The Stinky Cheese Man, the text is wafted and melted by the awful 'funky smell' which emanates from the eponymous character. In Jack's Story the text gets smaller and smaller as Jack repeats his story in an attempt to send the Giant to sleep. Early in the story he comments on the typography used for the Giant's voice: 'Could you please stop talking in uppercase letters? It really messes up the page.' These and many other visual jokes with words and text can offer further discoveries and investigations for a class of intrepid literary detectives. The relationship between the form and the content of the text can add more possibilities for imaginative writing, inviting the young artist to think further about the presentation of their ideas. These visual games come most completely into their own in the illustrations which tell their own version of a story alongside the text.

Reading images

From an art-historical perspective the execution of the illustrations in the two books is as subversive and boundary breaking as is the text itself. The majority of the illustrations were rendered in oil paint, a technique which dates back to the ancient world. However, Lane Smith's work contrasts with the highly finished and realistic effects created by many of his oil-painting predecessors. He uses the medium in a different and revolutionary way, scraping and splattering, splodging and blotting the surfaces of his paintings. The skin of the Frog Prince in *The Stinky Cheese Man* is blotted and blown as if rendered through a straw, imitating the watery lily pad which is his home, and is reminiscent of the work of artists such as Debuffet who uses muted, earthy and natural tones: gritty browns, blood reds, mustard-yellow ochres and dark seaweed greens.

The painted world which Smith creates is the kind of dreamscape also found in the work of Georgia O'Keeffe and European surrealists. His references to these artists extend the challenging, revolutionary and metafictive elements of his illustrations even further. Like the cubists and surrealists, Smith's works react against tradition. They extend the possibilities of painting and art as illusion to meet the demands of an ever-changing and fast-developing late twentieth-century world. The full-page illustration of Chicken Licken in *The Stinky Cheese Man* can be compared to Picasso's *Weeping Woman* and *Guernica* in which the facets of the face have been carved up and the features rearranged, placing eyes, mouth, nose or beak one upon the other. In each case, the resulting images are both disconcerting and aggressive. The images hold important clues about the text and as Helen Bromley reports in 'Spying on picturebooks', in *Talking Pictures*, children are particularly skilled at reading these non-verbal gestures and devices. Commenting on her work exploring intertextuality in picture-books with 6- and 7-year-olds, she reveals:

> There is no doubt in my mind that young children can successfully identify intertextual links of both a written and illustrative nature. . . . The experience underlined for me the sophistication of children today who bring to school vast experiences of reading visual texts. These are skills which, as teachers, we ignore at our peril. If we work with the grain, building on children's skills and knowledge, then we too will be able to 'take upon us' the mysteries that are the literacies of the future.
>
> (Bromley 1996: 111)

Conclusion

Both the text and the pictures in *The True Story* and *The Stinky Cheese Man* challenge and subvert established forms of storytelling by introducing new perspectives. Author and illustrator create their own versions of traditional and well-known stories and, in so doing, challenge the reading experience itself. In the worlds of Sciezska and Smith nothing is stable or concrete: the perpetual movement and energy is reminiscent of the multitude of images and ideas which bombard children every time they switch on the television, watch a film or play on the computer. In the postmodern world which today's children inhabit, the boundaries between real and unreal are constantly changing and being redefined. With the introduction of new media technologies such as satellite television, virtual reality, the internet, video games and cyber-space, the child of the late twentieth century has new and sophisticated encounters with visual texts and images. In the hands of artists like Sciezska and Smith definitions of literature and literacy are being challenged in the light of these changing experiences. In the words of Margaret Meek:

> Literature however defined or acquired or used or sought is never static. As language and art it changes and is changed by those who find uses for it and who, like the artists who create new books for children, actively seek to play the games of reading and writing and change the rules.
>
> (Meek 1991: 238)

The True Story and *The Stinky Cheese Man* can be used to show young readers that texts function on different levels and incorporate a wide range of complex narrative and visual devices. By looking closely at the pictures and text, and by asking questions about the way in which they have been made, the teacher can help children to appreciate and understand how these pictorial, literary and narrative devices produce their effects. Both of these books shatter any assumption that the picture-book's format and content, and its reliance on visual images to tell a story, makes it a 'simple read'. Our fast-changing modern world demands that the reader become an increasingly sophisticated and active interpreter. Metafictive picture-books can empower young readers by drawing on what they already know; and, as McCallum has noted, '[B]y involving readers in the production of textual meanings, metafictions can implicitly teach literary and cultural codes and conventions, as well as specific interpretative strategies' (McCallum 1994: 297).

These texts provide exciting, humorous and innovative retellings, and contain intertextual references to both traditional and postmodern popular culture. The discoveries and adventures contained within them can delight and inspire both pupil and teacher alike and expand the definitions of literacy today.

Note

1   I am grateful to Tiffany Astle and her class of 6-year-olds at Elsworth CE Primary School, Cambridgeshire, for providing me with examples of their work based around *The True Story of the Three Little Pigs*.
2   We regret that permission was not granted to reproduce some of the artwork from Scieszka and Smith's picture-books.

References

Bromley, H. (1996) 'Spying on picturebooks: exploring intertextuality with young children', in Victor Watson and Morag Styles (eds), *Talking Pictures*, London: Hodder & Stoughton.

Doonan, J. (1991) 'Reading new books', *Signal*, vol. 64.

Lewis, D. (1992) 'Looking for Julius: two children and a picture book', in K. Kimberley, M. Meek and J. Miller (eds), *New Readings. Contributions to an Understanding of Literacy*, London: A. & C. Black.

McCallum, R. (1994) 'Metafictions and experimental work', in P. Hunt (ed.) *The International Companion Encyclopaedia of Children's Literature*, London: Routledge.

Meek, M. (1991) *On Being Literate*, London: Bodley Head.

Scieszka, J. and Smith, L. (1989) *The True Story of the Three Little Pigs*, London: Puffin.

—— (1992) *The Stinky Cheese Man and Other Fairly Stupid Tales*, London: Puffin.

Sendak, M. (1988) *Caldecott and Co.: Notes on Books and Pictures*, London: Reinhardt in association with Viking Books.

Chapter 8

Reading the movies
Learning through film

Sarah Jones

As resources for education, film and video have long been regarded as poor relations of literature, and of drama in particular. There is a tendency to associate the watching of films with fun and frivolity and a lack of interest in exploring this medium further as a serious and effective way to teach the basics of literacy. All too often teachers who will use a video screening of, for example, *The Secret Garden* fail to benefit from the exciting richness of this resource because of insufficient viewing preparation, unspecific task-setting and lack of post-screening discussion. Without such extraneous activities the screening will be, at best, forgettable and, at worst, misleading and confusing for the students. Why are some parts of the story told in the book missing from the film? Why are scenes in an order different from that in the book? Why did the script use this word instead of that used in the book? Simple questions with interesting answers which, if explored to the full, can only add and bring life to the student's appreciation of the written word.

While film is perceived as a competitor to literature it will surely lose out. Not until it is celebrated as a means of building on the diversity of language, as a unique and powerful means of communication, and as an art form in its own right, will film find its rightful place in today's education system.

Thankfully this is beginning to happen as individual teachers embrace opportunities to exploit the potential of the moving image, but there are many barriers still to cross. Training and education for teachers in both practical and theoretical aspects of film and television remain woefully inadequate even though the British Film Institute, among others, is establishing a new programme to address this urgent need. Additional resources are desperately needed, with support and guidance on how these may be used.[1]

It seems to be generally assumed that the traditional literacy skills of reading and writing are on the decline, while visual texts predominate with the young today. Unfortunately, the challenge, variety and richness of many visual texts, and the fascinating ways children engage with them, are not widely valued in contemporary society, although some educators are becoming increasingly aware of their potential for young readers. Even so, there is a real danger that unless children are given the tools and taught the skills with which to analyse this discourse, some will fall prey to the remit of commissioners, broadcasters and film-makers, not to mention politicians and celebrities, who court the mass media for their own ends.

Most teachers would agree that today's young find films accessible and familiar, and are able to explore their meanings with highly personal reference points. It is believed that the stage at which young people recognise what they already know about film is the point at which they begin to engage with the medium and explore further. The meanings they, and we, derive from those images alter according to the context in which they are found, and it must be acknowledged that film can play a role in establishing our place in society and our sense of self. It does this by projecting back at us some of the things we think, feel and believe; often it reinforces perceptions, sometimes it challenges them.

And in a society increasingly dominated by the moving image – from advertising, TV, cinema, and, now, the Internet – children are likely to draw conclusions about the world around them increasingly from the images and sounds they see and hear on screen. Too often, debates about the influence of the media on children concern themselves with the harmful effect that images may have on them. We should consider also the less obvious but equally unsatisfactory effect that constant images of conventional relationships, class and gender distinctions, culture clashes, etc. may have on any child.

> The view of young people as the 'dupes' of popular media has a long history, and is regularly espoused by critics of all political persuasions. For many on the Right, the media are often seen as a major cause of moral depravity and violence; while they are routinely condemned by many on the Left for their reinforcement of racism, sexism, consumerism and many other objectionable ideologies. What unites these otherwise very different views is a notion of young people as helpless victims of manipulation, and as extremely vulnerable and impressionable.[2]

Makers of moving images have their own agenda, whether of entertainment, commerce or political gain; we as educators should open our children's eyes to this fact and, without spoiling their enjoyment of the magic, we should aim to encourage discernment and critical debate in viewers from an early age. Children have the right to make choices about the programmes and films they watch, and to understand the messages being conveyed; this will encourage them to develop into active, powerful interpreters of visual texts rather than risk them turning into passive consumers of the visual media.

This chapter does not set out a demand that all teachers incorporate film into their classroom teaching; it simply explores why this might be a useful exercise, while ensuring that we acknowledge and understand the choices available to us and our children. Film and video offer a wonderful resource for accessing diverse cultures and subjects, examples of which are given later in the chapter. Our children are familiar with many of the formats used by film-makers and associate them with fun. However, film conveys those cultures and subjects in a language all its own, a language which needs to be learnt and understood by teachers before being brought into the classroom. It is my hope that this chapter may both persuade teachers at primary level of the importance of teaching visual literacy skills, while also indicating through a few examples of good practice, and with training, preparation and access to resources, how straightforward and rewarding the use of film may be.

Reading the frame

It is important to remember that a film is a premeditated selection of images, put together in such a way as to successfully communicate the intent of the film-maker – be it to tell a simple story or to politically motivate. It is also worth bearing in mind that these categories may overlap: no Hollywood narrative is devoid of ideology; and dictators such as Hitler and Franco recognised the power of film in galvanising the 'masses'. It can hardly be denied that the conventional Hollywood blockbuster, from D. W. Griffith's *Birth of a Nation* of 1915 to Steven Spielberg's 1998 *Saving Private Ryan*, presents and preserves a stereotypically conservative, western view of the world. Film-making norms were established in America soon after the launch of the film industry, in 1895, and deviations from accepted practices in terms of subject matter and technical presentation have always been considered subversive and marginal. It is an all-too-familiar vicious circle of dependencies, with audience figures justifying producers' relentless outpourings of conventional images, while audiences decry the lack of choice and stimulation. The steady dumbing-down of the film-going public is sadly leading to a decline in experimental film-making which dares to open our eyes to new ways of thinking and seeing.

If we are to encourage our children to become discerning viewers we ourselves need in the first instance to get beyond the 'like/dislike' factor. *Why* didn't you like it? *What* was boring about it? *Which* were the best and worst characters and events? *What* did you like or not like about them? Keep asking yourself questions.

Always watch the film more than once. The first time is to enjoy it, to get 'the whole picture'; after all a film is not made to be analysed, but to tell a story, to communicate a message. Identify that message. Consider whether that is what the film is really about. Acknowledge the difference between retelling the story to check that facts have been understood, and articulating the themes which were the original premise for the film and for which the story – the narrative – is simply the vehicle.

Watch a second, third and fourth time, with specific aims in mind. Note down anything striking about the performances, costumes, make-up, hair design, props and locations. Then look out for colour, lighting, sound and music. Why did Spielberg decide to start off *Schindler's List* in colour and then change to black and white? How does he create this transition? The little girl in the red coat is then the only source of colour for almost three hours. What is the significance of her red coat? Red for danger, death, passion, but more than that. We see her through Schindler's eyes at certain key moments. The coat seems to represent the humanising of a man who until this point seemed only to be interested in girls, wine and money. This colour helps us to understand the man, to empathise with him and keep track of his development; at the same time it drives the narrative along.

Finally, learn to put yourself in the place of the camera operator so that you become aware of the way he or she uses the camera, moves it, changes the focus, redirects the angle, creates a new space. As with other visual media, film-making proceeds frame by frame, shot by shot, scene by scene, and nothing within those spaces will be superfluous to the message being conveyed. What the director has chosen to leave out can be as important as what he or she has included; the film represents choices made, a choices which are then denied to the viewer whose gaze is directed this way and that by the use of a close-up here, a change in focus from one character to another, a pan movement of the camera across the landscape, and so on.

But what of editing, cutting, montage? This is the painstaking postproduction process which gives pace, rhythm and life to a film. The average shooting–inclusion ratio of a film is approximately 10:1 which means that for every shot included in the final cut, there are nine lying on the cutting-room floor (or discarded in a computer's memory, depending on the technology used). This notion of selection and manipulation are added to when you consider how sense can be made of a sequence differently depending on the order in which you present the actions. The camera has been regarded as a means for replicating reality; yet how true-to-life can film be, given the number of choices a film-maker has to make. Even the most realistic documentary has been affected by choices of camera angle, focus and movement, lighting, editing, sound and so on.[3]

Examples of good practice

The aim of the film literacy projects set up by the education department at Cambridge Arts Cinema was to exploit the knowledge of and familiarity with film already possessed by children, while building on these elements to create valuable and enjoyable learning experiences for them. The workshops either concentrate on film itself in an attempt to start to raise awareness of the way in which images and sounds are constructed into stories and messages, or they take film as a starting-point for accessing another culture or subject, such as natural history. In both cases, there is a need to develop the skills required to understand how the stories, information and messages are communicated by the film-maker, and received by the audience, and each of the activities considered in the case studies which follow is designed to this end. They require no prior knowledge of film or film-making on the part of the student, and only basic awareness on the part of the teacher. What is essential is the enthusiasm to try out a new way of engaging with literacy.

Case study 1: James and the Giant Peach

The emphasis in this workshop is on 'screening stories' – how narrative may be conveyed using images and sound, rather than the written word – and how a book is transferred to screen.

This project came about due to the celebrations of the centenary of cinema, which in the UK took place in 1996. While the local multiplex played host to a week of jam-packed free screenings of the latest blockbusters, the education department at Cambridge Arts Cinema, realising it was in no position to compete, decided to devise and offer something different, something more akin to its aim of promoting visual literacy.

During one week in October 1996, we visited seven different primary schools in Cambridgeshire and delivered in each a two-and-a-half-hour session which incorporated both theory and practical work. The starting-point was the wonderful animated version of *James and the Giant Peach* by the director of *The Nightmare Before Christmas*, Tim Burton. We adapted video and written resources on this created and produced by Film Education (see note 1) in order to present the theoretical aspects of ordering (editing) and adaptation. The students watched short clips of the film, carefully chosen to illustrate key points from the previous discussion, and watched a video on which the director talked about his ideas for the film. All the time, we were trying to demystify the film-making process, encouraging the children to acknowledge that it takes a great deal of time, skill, people and money to make a movie, without wanting to ruin their enjoyment of the magic of cinema – a delicate balance!

The second part of the workshop moved the children into a period of intensive practical activity which tested their groupwork skills to the extreme. In teams of four or five, they had to devise an episode of film using the narrative structure of *James and the Giant Peach*, showing a character in a place he hates, moving through places he dislikes, towards the place he is searching for; in effect, to create a storyboard, characters and background, and then 'animate' it using a very basic camcorder. The aim was never to produce a quality film, merely to complete the process and play back the finished product, partly to prove to the children that they could achieve such a task, but also to enable them to see through the creation of a film from idea to screen. Writing was kept to a minimum, for two main reasons; first, to encourage less-able students; and second, to keep the emphasis on the image. Often the children found their ideas in films or programmes regularly watched, or other parts of their daily culture such as football teams. Most rewarding were their enthusiasm and ability to experiment with the artwork and objects around them to create special effects – visual and aural – such as those they would expect from films at the cinema.

The teacher needs very little technical expertise in order to recreate this workshop. Resources required are a camcorder, a tripod and a TV. The camera is kept totally still and the characters move around within the frame set up. To create movement, to 'animate' the characters, you simply need to think about how many seconds you wish each shot to be. Of course, an animation camera would take 24 frames per second, while a camcorder is much less sophisticated, but this should not be seen as a disadvantage. To use the former would require so much more time as to make the exercise impracticable; the children want to see 'their' film at the end of the session. Invariably, they were delighted by the animation effect achieved, however basic.

Case study 2: Microcosmos – the insect world in the frame

This delightful seventy-minute film tells the 'story' of a day in the life of a summer meadow 'somewhere in France'. It is not a documentary and there is no dialogue, simply the most beautiful and entertaining images of the world of such insects as snails, ladybirds, dung beetles and pond skates. It raises more questions than it answers, and will inspire the imagination of any viewer, young or old. It was painstakingly shot over two years with a specially-designed robotic camera and is set against a compelling soundtrack which adds emotion and resonance to the often brutal actions of the tiny creatures.

Microcosmos was released in the UK in May 1997, and was the subject of a major primary-school project co-ordinated by the Cambridge Arts Cinema. Teachers were first of all invited either to attend a preview screening at the cinema or to borrow a video copy of the film, so as to be able to prepare their pupils adequately for a quite unusual experience. The afternoon screening for schools was packed, with over 200 children from five different schools in and around Cambridge attending. On good advice, we approached a Cambridge University lecturer in entomology to give an introduction to the film, and he accepted with a certain degree of trepidation! In fact, his short performance was superb, complete with very accurate imitations of fighting dung beetles, and set the scene perfectly for the next seventy minutes.

We asked the teachers to consider setting the pupils the task of writing a short piece about the film, expecting a return of just one or two essays from each school. The result, however, was astounding, with most of the schools submitting bound collections of essays and drawings which clearly demonstrated the amount the children had gained from watching *Microcosmos*. These collections were, quite unexpectedly, to prove of great help to us in persuading a major sponsor to support an outdoor screening of the same film in the centre of Cambridge. The sponsor had been worried that the film might be 'unsuitable' for children!

Case study 3: *Imagery and* Romeo and Juliet

Baz Luhrmann's *Romeo and Juliet*, released in 1997, although not altogether the most appropriate film for use with primary-school age children, may be used to demonstrate how text and film can be studied at the same time to the benefit of each.

The aim would be to look at how the imagery of the written text contributes to our understanding of the characters and their relationships, how it highlights themes within the play and, also, how it can advance the plot. The film-maker uses the language of film – camera work, setting, costumes, music – as well as some of the text itself, to convey much of this information to the audience. By looking at one or more scenes from *Romeo and Juliet* (the written and the film texts), it is possible to discover the different ways in which meaning is constructed for an audience.

This session, adapted from material provided by Film Education, encourages students to read a short extract from the play beforehand and discuss what Shakespeare has Romeo say upon seeing Juliet for the first time (Act i, Scene v, lines 41–52). What colours and objects are referred to? What images do they conjure up? What feelings? Having elicited key words and phrases from the students, a clip of the same section from the 1997 film could be shown. Consider in particular what the film-maker has done to Shakespeare's text. Why has he reduced it to almost nothing? What has the film-maker used instead of words to convey to the audience the impact Juliet has on Romeo? Look at the clip (lasting about two minutes) several times and make notes on the setting, costume, design, location, lighting, music and camera work.

This exercise should help the students realise that meaning can be communicated in ways other than through dialogue alone, and that a film adaptation of a book or a play will never be quite the same as the original.

Conclusions

Although there are many exciting initiatives within the world of film education, cinema and teaching professionals tend to remain wary of each other.

Delegates attending a recent conference on Black British Film bemoaned the lack of interest in their work, and yet education and audience develop-ment were interestingly omitted from the strategies and solutions discussed. How are our children going to become interested in the more challenging 'difficult' films if they have not learnt the language of film? We have to take responsibility for their development of the skills of visual literacy if we are to expect them to enthusiastically change their viewing habits.

In France, film education is compulsory, and support is given by the Ministries of Education and Culture for a nationwide programme of cinema visits for all students at primary and secondary levels. Film is creeping its way into the curriculum in this country, but there is still a way to go before the official stamp of government approval is granted for incorporating it into primary-school teaching. More basic training is needed, ideally within the BEd and PGCE courses themselves, so that teachers feel at ease with this ever-changing medium. However, it is worth bearing in mind that although the new technologies may seem daunting, exciting work can be produced with the most basic equipment – TV and video player, cardboard frames and storyboards. And if you can teach yourself how to use a video camera, all the better. The children may seem to know more than us about the technology itself, but most still need to be taught how to make the most of it, enjoy it to the full, and become active, critical viewers. Teach them to turn off!

Notes

1   For further details contact the Regional Education Officer at the BFI, 21 Stephen Street, London, tel. 020–7255 1444. Film Education at Alhambra House, 27–31 Charing Cross Road, London, WC2H 0AU, tel. 020–7976 2291, run teacher training courses at primary and secondary levels and provide a range of film-related classroom resources. Your local independent cinema will probably run courses and hold seminars, especially if they are part of the COMEX network.
2   Buckingham, David and Sefton-Green, Julian (1994) 'Making sense of the media: from reading to culture', in *Cultural Studies Goes to School: Reading and Teaching Popular Media*, London: Taylor & Francis.
3   I would recommend the excellent new publication by Kevin Jackson (1998), *The Language of Cinema*, Manchester: Carcanet Press, which provides entertaining, accurate and comprehensible definitions of many of the terminology used in film-making. Clearly, it is not necessary for you to know them to any great extent – this is not about blinding the students with scientific knowledge – but the more you understand yourself about how the moving image is constructed, the better you will be able to interpret this in deconstructing those images to your students.

Chapter 9

'My mum's favourite yoghourt is "Diet Choice"'

Language study through environmental texts

Holly Anderson

Imagine you are 3 years old and walking down the High Street with your mum, or even younger being pushed in a buggy. All around you in every shop, at eye level, are brightly coloured posters, notices, adverts and bill-boards proclaiming the goods on offer. Even the funeral parlour has FAMILY BUSINESS and PRIVATE CHAPEL OF REST displayed discretely alongside the pictures of bluebell glades and seascape sunsets. The world is a maze of printed matter: colourful, mesmerising.

Now visualise the scene at home when the new Argos catalogue arrives. Pages are hurriedly flicked through until the toy section is located. Old hands know that the toys lie near the end of the catalogue; some may consult the index to find the appropriate pages. However, even a random search quickly produces results as photographs of Barbie, Disney characters and Action Man are all prominently displayed, their names written along-side in bold eye-catching type, using garish colours and the manufacturers' logo to ensure the products are instantly recognised by brand. Similarly clothing catalogues are scanned for the latest fashion and designer items, with logos highly visible both on the items and elsewhere on the pages to guarantee that choice is influenced not only by the look of the garment but by its design origin. Even very young children seem to be aware of the power of the logo, and choice is influenced by this. Older children may glance at the price, which is also quite dominant in terms of print size and layout, as that will be immediately referred to by the adult who is asked to foot the bill!

Children learn about the significance of print in our society by seeing how it is used by all those around them, and are often initiated into the numer-ous ways it functions by helping the adults, or those more experienced, per-form those functions. Choosing a card for nanny, signing kisses, watching the address being written, sticking on the stamp, all help build up a picture of one literate event: the written sending of greetings to someone we love.

Early years' teachers involved in the National Writing Project in the 1980s noticed the extent to which children were influenced by the wealth of print in their environment and by literacy practices in the home.

Examples of experimentation with Chinese script, musical notation, shopping lists and maps were provided for teachers by the children in their nurseries. These were often written on scraps of paper, not intended for any audience; they were self-initiated, executed for pleasure and often discarded in corners or in the waste bin where they would be found at the end of the school day, their purpose fulfilled (see National Writing Project 1989). Teachers have successfully built on such examples to develop literacy in the classroom (see Miller 1996). One teacher organised letters from the ladybird featured on the classroom wall to be sent to the children, who in turn replied in kind (see Hall 1989). Role play areas have been set up to take advantage of the myriad printed matter that children encounter, for example in the kitchen at home, in the library or in the office (see Campbell 1992).

Bringing the world of the child into the classroom makes sense for a number of reasons. It gives the new entrants security, as objects with which they are familiar bridge home and school. It gives children a chance to talk about things they know and care about. Moreover, it starts from the assumption that children know about print from a position of competence rather than from a deficit model where knowledge is 'stuffed' into them. Jo Weinburger, in her study (1996) of over forty parents from different backgrounds, found that nearly half deliberately pointed out examples of environmental print to their children even before nursery age and in addition noted that:

> the child was integrally involved with what the adults were doing. This was often by default rather than by design. For instance, if the parents were to go shopping, to the doctor's, to cook, write letters or bills, read letters and so on, this often had to be done with the child, or not get done at all.
>
> (Weinburger 1996: 18)

The current concern about boys' underachievement in English may be partially addressed by drawing on early literacy experiences, as they offer a supplement to the range of non-fiction genres available in the classroom. A recent QCA document focused on how to raise boys' achievements in English and recommends that curriculum provision should take into account a:

> curriculum with a heavy bias towards literature and fiction in particular is unlikely to appeal to many boys. English teaching should include a greater number and range of non-fiction texts. The features of different kinds of texts, and strategies for reading and writing them, should be explicitly taught.
>
> (QCA 1998: 6)

Helen Arnold (1996: 173) writes that 'a whole curriculum could be built around labels and notices'; similarly, Whitehead points out that:

> In terms of linguistics, such materials provide information about the features of letters, spaces, words and text and allow important insights into the symbols and sound correspondences of the alphabet. Furthermore, these materials are easily collected, easily replaced and perfect for endless play and manipulation.
>
> (1997: 165)

So environmental texts are a rich source for language study. Any number of such materials can be used to help children appreciate how texts work: the overall structure and purpose of the text as well as grammatical and lexical features of written language. The National Literacy Strategy, currently influencing practice in primary schools in the UK, encourages teachers to support children's reading and writing at text, sentence and word levels. This chapter explores ways in which environmental texts, often readily available in the home, can be used alongside fiction and poetry to help children become literate.

Brochures and catalogues provide a starting-point. Here there is much to talk about, even well before the child can read the captions let alone the fine print: Who knows what type of book it is? What is it for? Who has one at home? Who has used one? Travel brochures and catalogues, like picture-books, will have covers which rely heavily on pictorial images and only minimally on words. The front cover tends to be quite different both from the back cover and from the frontispiece, each having a particular function to perform. The layout of each page is a feast of pictures, captions and special offers. Travel brochures proclaim: 'Kids Go Free'; 'stay three nights and have one extra'; 'Bargain Basement'; 'Disney World'. These captions may be written in capital or lower-case letters, or a mixture, in different fonts and colours, but each is boldly displayed in letters large enough to catch the eye.

Unlike a picture-book, though, on a brochure or catalogue there is no author acknowledged, although the company's name will be prominent. Nevertheless someone, probably a whole team of people, will have written and produced the book with the sole purpose of enticing the reader to buy.

In such materials we can find the requisites for initiating a critical approach to reading. Becoming media-literate is vital in a world in which we are surrounded by images meant to persuade. Wray and Lewis, reflecting on critical literacy, suggest the examination of pictures and layouts, as well as written language:

> All texts are located in a particular set of social practices and understandings. They involve choices. Critical reading involves an explicit

examination of these choices and hence the particular social understandings and values underlying texts.

(1997: 104)

Long before children can read between the lines occupied by the written
word, they can discuss the way the whole visual package has been selected
to show the product in its most positive light. This may open up a debate
about whether such images do in fact give a fair depiction of the product
inside, as many children will have experienced the disappointment of finding
that the actual item falls short of its represented quality. So looking at the
front cover alone can open up a whole range of issues, with adverts from
magazines and the television being used to extend the discussion of presentation of products. Cathy Pompe (1996) has provided excellent examples
of very young children, already skilled at reading media images, learning
about media texts by designing their own packages and adverts.

This is a very important feature of work at the whole-text level, but
actual page layout, too, including structure and organisation, needs to be
discussed. The different ways we read fiction and non-fiction (indeed the
multitude of reading practices) should be made explicit to children. Brochures and catalogues have features in common with other informative
texts which can be highlighted by sampling. The headings on the contents
page (for example 'Fashion' and 'Footwear' sections, which in turn are subdi-
vided into women's, men's and children's) have an important lexical
function as they convey the generic category to which each item belongs.
Children draw on what they know about the products to sort and categorise
them; whereas for beginning readers, who might hunt for particular items
in the index, knowledge of alphabetical order is reinforced and their attention drawn to initial phonemes and the graphemes which represent them.

Inventive teachers can therefore use such texts to teach initial sounds.
Pictures of sports clothes sorted according to brand can be compiled
by sifting through mail order catalogues, and the children encouraged to
predict which brand is to be searched for by the teacher saying the initial
sound, holding up the initial letter, or even clapping the syllables contained
in the word – Is it Ad – i – das or Ree – bok? Such activities are planned
to support different stages of phonological development, helping children
to distinguish between sounds, to hear syllabic components and to
link graphemes with phonemes. So work at lexical and sub-lexical levels
is possible using catalogues, with page after page of products providing
opportunities to look at words, letters and fonts. Examination of the wide
range of print used will clarify other techniques which help the reader:
prices, sizes, descriptions, lists, reference numbers and section headings,
with the boldest print reserved for the categories and products themselves.
Page numbers and even colour-coded pages help orientate the reader to
the products on offer. The skilled teacher intervenes, questions and listens,

thus enabling the child to think through what she or he knows about these items. It is such modelling by an experienced reader which helps scaffold the child's understanding of how information is displayed and retrieved.

Favourite food packages can be used in similar ways in the classroom to help children think about the structure of texts: the range of print, for example on the cereal boxes contained in a variety pack, is quite stunning (see Figure 9.1). Although the youngest children will be unable to read the fine print, discussions about the front and back of each box, their functions and their differences, will draw on what the children know about the products. Much has been written (see e.g. Campbell 1992) on the way very young children can pick out letters which mean something to them: the McDonald's 'M' is often cited as one of the first written symbols which children seem to identify with ease, even from some considerable distance. The distinctive 'K' in Kellogg's makes boxes containing the company's cereals instantly recognisable to children. The fronts of cereal packets, their large bold lettering kept to a minimum, identify the contents and the brand, as also do the distinctive logos, colours and their overall design.

A collection of cereal packets can be sorted by brand, with young children spotting all the distinctive 'kicking Ks' on boxes of Kellogg's cereals, or by contents with digraphs, such as *ch* in choco and *sh* in shredded, being familiar through use. The more expert reader will notice how conventions are broken to reinforce the logo (as in krispies) and punctuation marks (for example both the possessive apostrophe and the exclamation mark are very obvious on some cereals). Kellogg's variety boxes each have a different cartoon character, pictures of which are used to support the print in a way quite different from that in which illustrations extend an understanding of narrative. However, both rely on pictorial image *and* written word for an appreciation of the whole text, and by having minimal but essential and eye-catching information alongside the picture the manufacturer communicates with the intended audience to sell the product.

Each packet face contains different information; the structure and the layout (which are different again from those mentioned in the catalogue and brochure section) are also worth exploring. The breakdown of the food categories according to nutritional content (e.g. fats, carbohydrates, protein values, etc.) is arranged as a chart, whereas the actual ingredients are listed. Children can be easily encouraged to spot certain 'buzz' words: my reception class quickly learnt to find the word 'sugar' in the list of ingredients on food packages. Having had a visit from the dentist and done experiments to show that sugary drinks were bad for your teeth, the children astounded their parents by insisting on examining food packages at home to check whether sugar was one of the first ingredients listed (being aware of the significance of word order in indicating the proportion of an ingredient in the product). Moreover, key words and labels, for example 'low

Figure 9.1 Range of print styles featured on a cereal box from a variety pack.
Source: Copyright 1999 Kellogg Company.

fat', may be already familiar from home experiences, with one child delightedly pointing to a yoghourt which had 'Diet Choice' written on it, and exclaiming: 'That's my mum's favourite!'

I want to turn now to items which may have a shared authorship. Cards and invitations, for instance, rely on the sender to supply part of the written information. Food, celebrations and loved ones hold centre stage in any young child's world, and parties provide a whole range of literacy experiences, both for the provider and the recipient. My godson, 5 next week and in his first term at school, was eager to read out over the phone the list of names of the people he had invited to his party, recognising their names by the initial letters: 'That's J for Josua; same as me, but mine is Jo.' He had written his own name on each invitation, and because his mother had discussed each category with him (date, time and venue) as she filled in the details, he was able to 'read' the invitations to his friends when delivering them at school. He was also able to read their handwritten names on the replies and work out whether they were able to come to his party from the 'I can/I can't come' box.

A postbox in the classroom or a thoughtfully constructed role play area can extend such abilities, encouraging children to send notes and cards to each other. The children in my reception class frequently held teddy bears' picnics and pirate parties which involved designing and sending invitations and cards and much deliberation over what information to include. Teachers can employ such texts for early excursions into both morphology (*can/can't* come to your party), punctuation and grammar, and the use of apostrophes, as in the above example to denote contractions.

Many invitations feature gender-specific elements which are worth exploring at text level. Pink gingham check for Barbie or blue for Thomas the Tank Engine enable any 5-year-old to tell you instantly which is meant to appeal to girls and which to boys. While an in-depth discussion about gender stereotyping might not be of high priority in an early years' classroom, children's awareness of gender stereotypes may be extended to an early understanding of how manufacturers often draw on this awareness to sell their products. Similarly, making gender bias explicit to children helps them develop their own understanding of the power of pictorial image to persuade and reinforce cultural images and stereotypes. Again, by sorting a stack of old cards (an essential resource in a classroom) it may be possible to extract the birthday cards from the pile just by an examination of the illustrations. What features discriminate between birthdays and other celebrations? Are they all suitable to send to anyone? If not, what makes them appeal to different groups of people? Investigating such matters enables children to look at the semiotics of the card, to read the pictorial signs which give out messages to buyers and guide their choices.

Turning to the written text, birthday cards are useful as they usually contain a greeting, and often a verse. Young children, even those who are not yet able to read print, will see patterns in the layout, and print of different sizes to distinguish the poem from the greeting. The different fonts and sizes of capital letters used form part of the overall impression, and the layout of the text tends to be unlike the print in a storybook. Birthday rhymes in cards provide additional opportunities for reading verse aloud; and hearing rhyming sounds and predicting rhyming words are, of course, important building blocks in the initial stages of reading, as research documented in Bryant and Goswami (1990) and Goswami (1995) has shown.

Linking children's knowledge of sounds to the graphic representation of how the 'rime' in words may stay the same can be achieved using a random selection of children's birthday cards as these contain language which is rich in rhyme, rhythm and repetition. A zig-zag card with farm animals and the sounds they make (see Figure 9.2) is a perfect invitation to use speech bubbles and speech marks to denote reported speech, as well as a means of encouraging children to think of other verbs for noises and finding alliterative names for animals (such as Sharon Sheep). This gives children the perfect opportunity to hear similarities between words and to hear words that share the same initial or ending sounds. Thus phonological awareness and grapho-phonic relationships can be studied through such artefacts, with the teacher emphasising onset and rime as well as analogy (see Goswami 1995).

To become proficient writers the morphology of words also needs to be taken into account, and birthday cards can once more assist in this. Common features in such words as 'grandson', 'granddaughter' and 'granny' can be made explicit, so that children see how the prefix 'grand' is used to denote the relationship between grandparent and grandchild, and how 'grandmother' is abbreviated to 'granny' (or even nanny). Many children may well be able to recognise the whole word 'birthday', it being a highly significant word for them, and the root word 'day' also features in the names for days of the week. I remember the amazement of children in a reception class when they realised that once they could write 'day' they could attempt to write the name for any day of the week, especially if they could also remember the initial letter. (Amusingly, 'Thursday' and 'Friday' caused problems because the children's spoken language did not distinguish between the initial sounds: *Fur*sday and *Fri*day. Overcompensation at one point produced a rash of *Thur*sdays and *Thri*days.)

Making links between words through their root stem is even more important when the sound of the stem changes, as in *sign* and in*sign*ificant. Morphemes at the end of some words denote tense and singularity or plurality, and seeing the written form emphasises these links, going beyond a simple sound–symbol correlation. Farm animals mooing, bleating, oinking and neighing on birthday cards give an opportunity to focus on words ending in 'ing'. Plurals may sound as if they are written either with a *z* or an *s* (hear the difference when saying *pigs* and *ducks*), but the grammatical

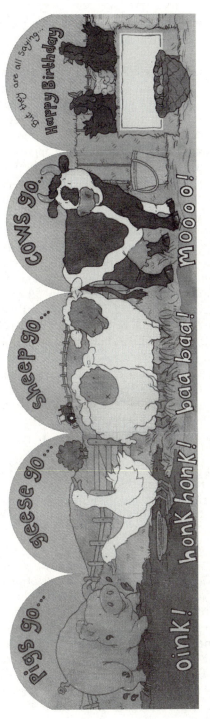

Figure 9.2 Birthday cards afford many opportunities for children to learn about words.

Source: Farmyard Greetings by Rachel O'Neill and N. E. Middleton, Camden Graphics Ltd.

system determines the way the words are constructed to show plurals, and it is this knowledge which enables us to go beyond a simple phonological connection to draw on morphological knowledge.

Emphasis on the way words are constructed to show meaning extends to focusing at sentence level on language as a written system, where grammatical knowledge is made explicit within a familiar context. The examples above provide opportunities for teachers to use or discuss terms such as 'verb', 'tense' or 'plural'. Other parts of speech, too, may be discussed in a shared context, where even the use of metalanguage can be natural and appropriate. Indeed part of the pleasure is in the use of long words, and far removed from grammar exercises and 'naming of parts'. A group of year-2 children told me with relish 'We're thinking about alliteration today!' as they searched for adjectives with the same initial letter as their names, like Ticklish Tyrone, or Merry Meera.

Nouns are mentioned as families of words are collected: uncle, son, nanny, mum, to name but a few to be found on birthday cards. Sub-lexical morphemic links are made between mum, mummy and mother, and these are opportunities to collect maternal names from other languages to see similarities and differences. Printed greetings in cards are usually quite succinct: sentences are often simple or compound, rhymes being short and glaringly obvious. Such predictable and unimposing language is accessible to young children, and links between reading and writing, fundamental to development of literacy, are made as children generate their own greetings and poems to add to those on the cards. Children draw on their knowledge of the way sounds are represented and words and sentences constructed, enabling terminology to be used in context and the grammatical rules governing the written system to be made explicit. All this from a few birthday cards!

These are beginnings of a lifelong interrogation of texts, in which the very youngest readers are encouraged to see the relationship between themselves, as readers, and the writing and its authors as a dynamic process. As Nick Jones so powerfully writes: 'Good readers come to know the instability of meaning, by knowing what bears upon the process by which meanings are made' (1991: 167).

Finally there is another advantage to consider when using environmental print to draw children's attention to the fine details of our writing system: such print is designed to be eye-catching and to stand alone. Many teachers are fearful that constant analysis of story texts may result in a stunting of children's appreciation of narrative; that getting lost in a book and the ability to hear the tune on the page will be adversely affected by dissection and scrutiny of the text. There are no such problems when using print in catalogues and on cereal packets for focused work; moreover the source material is readily available for recycling in this way. Teachers have always spread their nets wide when searching out suitable materials to use with children, and they should resist the current dominance of big books and having to rely on the texts the publishers have decided to make available. This is not to say that big books should not be considered an essential part of the reading diet of children; it is merely a plea that other texts should not to be forgotten.

Just as some children enjoy playing with numbers, the sheer joy in applying mathematical rules being what satisfies, so others take delight in manipulating the nuts and bolts of language, being comforted by a deepening understanding of the systems in operation and intrigued by finding a logic in seeming inconsistencies. Using environmental texts as a means to play with language should complement not replace literature in the centre of the stage, and may even allow more time for children to become immersed in narrative without always having to use it as a tool for language study.

References

Arnold, H. (1996) 'Penguins never meet polar bears. Reading for information in the early years', in D. Whitebread (ed.) *Teaching and Learning in the Early Years*, London: Routledge.

Campbell, R. (1992) *Reading Real Books*, Milton Keynes: Open University Press.

Goswami, U. (1995) 'Rhyme in children's early reading', in R. Beard (ed.) *Reading and Writing*, London: Hodder & Stoughton.

Goswami, U. and Bryant, P. (1990) *Phonological Skills and Learning to Read*, London: Lawrence Erlbaum Associates.

Hall, N. (ed.) (1989) *Writing with Reason*, London: Hodder & Stoughton.

Jones, N. (1991) 'Reader, writer, text', in R. Carter (ed.) *The LINC Reader*, London: Hodder & Stoughton.

Miller, L. (1996) *Towards Reading*, Milton Keynes: Open University Press.

National Writing Project (1989) *Becoming a Writer*, Walton-on-Thames: Nelson.

Pompe, C. (1996) '"But they're pink!" – "Who cares!": popular culture in the primary years', in M. Hilton (ed.) *Potent Fictions. Children's Literacy and the Challenge of Popular Culture*, London: Routledge.

QCA (1998) *Can Do Better: Raising Boys' Achievement in English*, Hayes: QCA Publications.

Weinburger, J. (1996) *Literacy Goes to School. The Parents' Role in Young Children's Literacy Learning*, London: Paul Chapman Publishing Ltd.

Whitehead, M. (1997) *Language and Literacy in the Early Years*, 2nd edn, London: Paul Chapman Publishing Ltd.

Wray, D. and Lewis, M. (1997) *Extending Literacy: Children Reading and Writing Non-Fiction*, London: Routledge.

Chapter 10

'And they lived happily ever after . . . not really!'

Working with children's dictated texts

Isobel Urquhart

Jay[1] is happily indifferent to reading and writing – the former is boring, and the latter a chore – but he remains good-humoured about our puzzling insistence that he do something about it. What really matters to Jay is doing scientific experiments, although he will concede that it is unfortunate that he cannot record his observations or explain in writing what he has learnt. Best of all, though, is going fishing with his grandad, in whose company Jay is an avid learner, having no problems tackling new vocabulary or complex skills.

During the Literacy Hour, the teacher has given Jay's group an adapted writing task of fifteen minutes' duration to be undertaken independently. For this particular series of lessons, Jay (aged 9) is targeted for individual help. In the first session, his scribe is a parent. First of all she talks to Jay about his fishing experiences, and then takes down his dictated story about going fishing the previous weekend. Jay likes dictating to his scribe. She lives near the school and seems to understand his way of putting things. She refrains from stopping to correct him, and does not suggest her own ideas. She knows the places that he talks about, and he feels that he is having a dialogue with her more than dictating to her. To his surprise, Jay finds that he has dictated a whole page of text. 'Am I going to have to read all that?' he asks, but you can tell that he is quietly impressed that his story takes up so much room when it is written down. Jay has never managed to write more than about four lines himself – in big writing. Afterwards, the scribe types up the story in a layout that looks like a proper book – page numbers, appropriate size and style of font, for example. She types the words he actually said, adding only some basic punctuation to reflect the meaning he intended.

You thread your line first through all the eyes on the fishing rod. After you've threaded the line, you put your float on. The float is for when the fish bites the hook – the float goes under. The fish bites the maggot, which is on the hook, and then the hook goes in its lip and the float goes under. The float also helps you cast out into the river, and it has weights on it to help it get out further. Then you have to put your weights on and the hook. And a maggot.

You have to buy the maggots from the fishing tackle shop. You buy them in fifty-pence lots, and they last about two or three days. Usually I keep them in the garden. They're in a tub and I put them in a corner.

(Extracted from Jay's story)

The next day, Jay reads back his own text to the scribe at a time when the rest of the class is doing individual work. He starts reluctantly – it seems so much to read, and he is so used to fluency and accuracy breaking down that he often loses interest. However, supported by his recollection of what he had dictated, allied to a natural interest in the subject matter – which is described using a vocabulary and syntax with which he is familiar – Jay finds himself reading with greater-than-usual fluency and accuracy. Jay is 'cool' about his new ability to read so well, but pleased in a dignified sort of way.

During the next group-work session, he is invited by his scribe to make changes to his text but is too pleased with his accomplishment to want to do that yet. So, the scribe invites him to dictate some more – either another story, or an extension to the existing story. Jay tells a story about the Christmas when his grandad bought him a new fishing rod. This also gets typed up and the two stories are put together into a book with spiral binding, so that more pages can be added later.

The next targeted session was a week later. In the meantime, Jay has taken a copy of his book home with him, and his grandad has praised him and listened to him read it, and told him the correct words to describe the different equipment they used. His grandad has bought Jay a big technical book on fishing which he brings to school and shows to the teacher, saying: 'Can I read this?' Jay's best friend Danny has also read Jay's story and said that it was OK, in a tight-lipped boys' way of showing enthusiasm, not wanting to show Jay up with too much praise. Danny and Jay ask if they can write a story together. A copy of Jay's story is put on display in the reading corner. It has stiff and laminated card covers designed by Jay, so that it does not get dog-eared. Jay has drawn pictures at home to go with the story, and these are inserted into the growing book. Other boys in the class think Jay's book looks good, and they read it, too, commenting on their own experiences of fishing, comparing Jay's commentary with those in other books. What more authentic experience of authorship can there be?

Becoming a reader and writer through dictated text

Integral to the encounter with quality texts, such as those described in this book, is that children are enabled to see the possibilities of personal meaning and a deeper, more discriminating, engagement with texts, their own and others', which makes reading and writing more than just an instrumental exercise.

At its most basic level, dictated texts enable children to sustain a meaningful narrative at much greater length than they would be able to write on their own, as Jay found out. With a scribe managing the technical aspects of writing, children do not just compose meaningful texts but complete their narratives and revise them. These are subsequently available as texts which the author, and other children, are genuinely interested in reading and which they therefore read more willingly and more accurately. Although the use of language experience approaches to develop children's literacy is not new, dictated stories continue to provide valuable opportunities for children to develop literacy skills at text, sentence and word levels. Moreover, they can be readily accommodated within current classroom practices and curricular guidance.

It is the opportunity which dictated stories give children to become increasingly discriminating authors of meaningful texts that is at the heart of this chapter. Allowing children to dictate a text makes an important statement: difficulties with technical aspects of writing should not be taken as evidence that a child cannot be an author with all the richness of personal autonomy and confidence in sharing one's knowledge, understanding, attitudes and feelings that that term implies (Smith 1994).

However, children who have difficulties with aspects of writing such as spelling, punctuation and handwriting often learn that others value these technical features of writing very highly. This is revealed to children in the ways we respond to their attempts to convey ideas in writing, and through the activities they undertake in English lessons. For some children, a relentless emphasis on the accurate recognition and production of words and sentences seems to be the only kind of reading and writing that they do. It is not surprising that endless drill activities, worksheets on phonic elements, spelling lists, and reading short amounts of 'denurtured text' lead children to infer that doing reading and writing in school is mostly about testing their performance of word-attack skills, and not about the communication of and involvement in meaning.

Our job as teachers is, of course, to ensure that all children's experience of reading and writing is sufficiently rich that, while paying attention to the basic skills, we also introduce them to the pleasures and the deep meanings to be obtained by engagement in meaningful literacy events. However, the fragmented experience of writing that a prescriptive pedagogy such as the Literacy Hour seems to encourage could easily prevent children from having the kinds of extended writing experience that foster such deep engagement. The problem is that when we get the balance wrong between appreciating children's meaningful communications and their technical correctness, children learn where our own, and society's, anxieties lie, anxieties they may replicate in narrow concerns of their own about spellings and presentation.

This can lead children to work very slowly at writing, partly through a wish to avoid a difficult task, but also because they take such enormous pains, at word level, concentrating on spellings, and handwriting, for example, afraid to take risks in conveying their ideas. The result is that these children often do not complete their writing tasks. This has serious effects on their perception of the act of writing: first, they rarely experience the sense of completion that is part of the satisfaction of writing; and second, responses to writing-in-progress tend to focus on editing and proofreading errors, rather than on the final presented meaning. This then reinforces these children's preoccupation with the technical correctness of writing.

Some children produce very small amounts of writing in the allotted time, even though they have worked and thought hard to produce their texts. It is very easy for busy teachers to make negative assumptions about what children know or can imagine, or about the extent of their writing vocabulary, from these meagre offerings. Trying to decipher meaning from a scrappy bit of badly spelt writing at the end of a busy day can impair our own ability to hear an author's voice!

In addition, what these children really know or think or feel is unknown to us. Some are cautious writers, avoiding words they cannot spell, or ideas that will be hard to hold on to while struggling to write a sentence or two correctly. The vital point, of course, is that for the most part the children have yet to acquire a capacity for reflection on their own meanings when they write, and so are themselves unaware of where their thoughts might take them, or how their ideas and feelings might change.

As Brigid Smith (1994) describes them, dictated texts act as bridges between children's fluent and confident spoken language and the 'frozen' language of written text, which cannot rely on the paralinguistic features of talk (gestures, shared context, non-verbal expressions) that help us fully understand a spoken text. They are also bridges between a child's actual and potential levels of performance. In this way, dictated stories exemplify Vygotsky's notion of the zone of proximal development, with an expert scribe drawing up the child-apprentice from his or her level of unassisted performance through contingent and scaffolded instruction and support to a level of potential achievement. One important example of this scaffolding is that the scribe models and makes explicit the importance of the communication of meaning, something that children anxious about spelling and handwriting find hard to focus on. In working with a scribe, children internalise aspects of the literacy task, both implicitly, in the kind of moment-to-moment intersubjectivity between scribe and writer, and explicitly, in the overt instruction given by experts (teachers, for example, sensitive to what the novice now needs to know or do in order to make progress).

It is the purpose of scribed texts to demonstrate to those dictating that they are authors by emphasising the composition and communication of meaning. Scribed texts can demonstrate a deeper understanding, a richer imagination, a more coherent sequence of thoughts than would a child's unsupported writing.

What can we teach through children's own texts?

Everything from concepts about print, the compositional aspects of writing, editing and proofreading, to genre characteristics can be taught using children's dictated stories (Smith 1994). Once a text has been produced, it becomes like any other text available for work at sentence and word levels. For example, the words that a child considers important in his or her own texts can be built into a family of similar words; grammatical features of past tenses can be identified and so on. In reading practice, children are more likely to use the full range of reading strategies, including semantics and syntax, in texts that reflect their own language use, and where the semantic fields are highly predictable.

The use of dictated texts has demonstrated that nearly all children can plan, compose and read texts, and in some cases these are more linguistically demanding than the books they have been assigned. What has been dictated can have a linguistic complexity beyond what assessments based on unsupported writing tasks indicate. Jay's motivated reading of his grandad's fishing text, despite his stumbling, show him attempting, sometimes correctly, to read complex sentences and unfamiliar vocabulary. In his scheme reader, such linguistic features are rarely present, and so provide little opportunity for children to learn how to read them. When Jay composes his own text, these differences are even more dramatic.

The dictated text, therefore, frees children from the often vain attempt to represent their thoughts in inadequate vocabulary and simple syntax, allowing them to engage into greater linguistic complexity in their spoken accounts of what they know. This is particularly noticeable when children are working in specific subject disciplines or constructing non-fiction genres such as argument or persuasion. Such structures are often very demanding for inexperienced writers, but in this context children can be seen to include implicitly understood features of written language. That is, when they are dictating, children do not simply speak as they would in conversation. While they construct their dictation partly within their existing under-standing and experience of written texts, they also experiment with the less familiar genres which make up the discourse of subject knowledge. This is not just a matter of learning some specialist vocabulary, but of acquaintance with, for example, the bigger shapes of what historians write about and how they write about it. It includes understanding how description, explanation and argument work, and how they are used within the subject. Children who begin to use the language genres of science or history in their writing and speaking are therefore taking an important step towards being scientifically or historically minded. By speaking their writing and then reading it back in the dictated text approach, children rehearse their entry into subject knowledge as it is structured within language.

Writing down words and stories, often to accompany pictures they have drawn, is for very young children a familiar activity in infant schools. Children readily understand how ideas and stories can be turned into writing and books. It is an essentially dialogic activity, where language and meaning are shared between the child and the adult scribe, and where the child learns the ways in which meaning can be 'frozen' into written text. Early concepts about print can therefore be explored with very inexperienced writers and readers in the course of the dictation. An inexperienced writer will watch the scribe very closely when he is writing, and observe many of the decisions that a writer has to make when turning spoken language into writing – punctuation in particular, but also when a scribe thinks aloud about authorial decisions (e.g. 'How is koi carp spelt?') or directs a question to the writer ('Do you want a new paragraph there?'), – and where discussions can be had about genre characteristics. For example, Kelly decided to set her story in the past, so she asked the scribe for the names of old coins. She realised that in this genre she had to avoid anachronisms in order to make the story sound authentic.

Dictated text exemplifies the strong links between reading and writing. In Frith's model of literacy development, advances in understanding the logographic, alphabetic and orthographic stages in reading and writing are asymmetrically assimilated, where reading or writing experiences alternately drive advances in the other skill (Frith 1985). Where teachers use the child's own text as the basis for learning to spell words that the child would like to be able to write, there are opportunities to exploit the importance of analogical skills between reading and writing, by building spelling families based on words that can be read from the child's own text (Goswami and Bryant 1990). Dictated texts can be used also to make cloze procedures which draw attention to particular word and syntactic features, the child having to decide what words are to be inserted in the spaces where the words have been blanked out.

The models of literacy that underpin the National Curriculum and the National Literacy Strategy describe a progression towards an optimal standard of achievement. Children's literacy is thus necessarily seen in deficit terms, and plotted according to developmental stages towards that standard of achievement. Gunther Kress, in his book *Before Writing: Rethinking the Paths to Literacy*, argues:

> It may be that the real focus of theory has always been on adult users and uses of language; and where the focus has been on children it has been in order to see how, or to demonstrate that they 'move into' the adult system.
>
> (Kress 1997: 88)

As in the case of Jay, it is quite possible to use dictated stories to help children make progress in their reading and writing according to these standards. However, their usefulness extends beyond skill acquisition, for there are particular features of children's dictated stories which speak to their and our deepest concerns. This often shows itself to be important when children are dealing, for example, with difficulties in their lives, such as transitions from school to school or family to family, or coming to terms with life-threatening illness. Therefore the next section explores the emotional significance of dictating stories for some children.

What does the dictated story mean to children?

Children are not just adults-in-progress and their story writing has a meaning and importance for them in terms not just of where it is leading (as in terms of achieving adult levels of accuracy and fluency) but of what it lets children say about how they see themselves now. That is, story writing forms one way for children to construct current meanings, making sense of reality, both interior and exterior, in the here-and-now of their lives. As Michael Rosen says in *Did I Hear You Write?* (1989): 'when we write something down, there's a bit of me there!', and the powerful thing about writing is that it has permanence and can be revisited and thought about over and over again. In this repeated reading of their own texts there seems to be for some children a pleasure that indicates some important mental engagement with the meanings they have created. Children write with the same kind of serious intentionality as all authors, particularly when they have a sense of personal commitment to the purpose and the audience of the writing.

Kress suggests that when we look at meaning-making from the child's point of view, we see a different picture: instead of seeing children as less than competent users of adult systems, 'we can see what it is they do to make their meanings in the absence of the routinised, practised, finely honed and quite "natural" competence of adults' (Kress 1997: 89). In terms of dictated fictions, this viewpoint reveals to us that children use linguistic and other criteria which are significant to them at that stage of their lives, and we see also that children's interests are transitory. 'Children's interest changes; and as it does, that which is regarded as criterial by the child about [making meaning in stories] changes; and so what is represented changes' (ibid.). In *Becoming a Reader* (1994) Appleyard comments on a change in children's reading tastes, suggesting that there is a general move away from fantasy to realism. Although Appleyard's argument distorts the variety of ways in which children develop as readers into a generalised linear progression, there might be evidence in children's writing of similar movements which are expressed as linguistic choices.

For example, there is evidence in Jedd's dictation of a fantasy in which he discovers a benevolent father-figure in the middle of the woods, of some disillusion with the appropriate fantasy ending as a narrative solution. We can see in the negotiation he conducts with his scribe how Jedd uses the criterion of real life to evaluate the fantasy narrative in comparison with his own experience; we can see also how he identifies features of writing, such as the typography, in which to show the emphasis he wants to make.

JEDD [dictating]: Next morning they got up and had a lovely big break-fast and then they all die.
SCRIBE: You want to finish the story now, do you? 'They lived sadly ever after?' 'Happily ever after'?
JEDD: Happily.
SCRIBE: You don't really believe it, do you?
JEDD: Yeah, well nothing finishes happily ever after do they? You know they use 'happily ever after' just because it sounds normal for a story. Whoever lived happily ever after? I'm still trying to. I haven't even lived happily yet.
SCRIBE: So do you want this story to end happily ever after?
JEDD: Yeah because people like it that way most of the time, don't they? Put 'not really'. Put 'not really' in capitals with lines, with lines under them.
SCRIBE: Okay, will I put an exclamation mark as well?
JEDD: Yeah – four is a bit too many, put three.

This negotiation is significant for understanding what children might be doing in the way of making meaning in their dictated fictions. Opportunities for children to write at length and to try out their new ideas about what is important in making meaning in stories is therefore a crucial experience for young readers and writers. What is particularly interesting about the dictated story is that the scribe provides the kind of intersubjective relationship that characterises much of our early learning. In this collaborative relationship, a child like Jedd can verbalise, and therefore make explicit to himself, some of his unarticulated ideas about the story.

And suddenly he heard a lot of trampling and crashing of leaves. Someone was walking towards him. It was his father. Tom felt pleased and exhilaratingly happy. He had just come back from France. He was an oil-worker, and he had a lot of money and he gave Tom £20 to give to his mum. So his father took Tom home. Tom's mum was very pleased to see him.

Next morning they got up and had a lovely big breakfast. And they lived happily ever after.

NOT REALLY!!!

(Extracted from Jedd's story)

This topic is discussed in more detail later in the chapter.

Gunther Kress's main concern is with linguistic features of children's written texts. However, in children's fictions, we notice that there often seems to be something important at an emotional and personal level for the child in some of the texts they write. As we know, we often construct the meaning of our lives within a narrative structure. When very young children play out narrative episodes ('Now, I'm telling the baby not to cry. Sally, you're the baby. Lie down there, and don't cry.'), they find in the imagination ways to make sense of themselves and the important events in their lives. Creating stories is a development from this early symbolising, so that writing stories can be thought of as a form of 'serious play' which remains an important part of children's emotional and cognitive development until beyond their infancy. Meek (1982) refers to the 'imaginative drive to cognitive function', while Steedman (1982) and Smith (1994) refer to the ways in which some writers fictionalise their own lives or otherwise invest emotional energy in the writing of the text. Many children are able to pursue this for themselves in their writing, and it is an important part of their emotional and cognitive development to be able to do so.

However, some children may be denied this opportunity because of their technical difficulties with writing. For these children, the scribe fulfils an important role, and one that can extend well beyond simply transcribing the child–author's dictation because she frees the child to dictate 'felt' texts of this kind. At first sight, what Kevin (aged 10) dictated appears from the extract, to be a violent and macabre story that would quite rightly worry us had we found a child writing this in the classroom.

Then Kevin bumped into Jason. Kevin cut his eye on Jason but was all right. Then Jason took out his razor-sharp knife and said, 'You can't get away from me, Kevin. Not from Jason, anyway. Ha, ha, ha, ha, ha.'

Then Kevin filled a bucket of water and threw it at Jason but it missed his face and hit his hand and he had the knife in it and melted Jason's hand off. And Jason was screaming and blood was everywhere. Then Kevin gets a wire, puts it in Jason's mouth and says, 'Eat this, you son of a bitch.'

And Jason's mouth puffs up and then it's puffed up so much – Bang! Jason's head's been blown off and it looks as if he's dead. Then Kevin's walking away, smiling in a cheeky way.

Then, 'Waaaagh!'

'I've got you, you know, Kevin, and do you know what I'm going to do to you? I'm going to blow your head off too, with my knife.'

Then Jason stabs his knife into the radiator and cannot get it out and above the radiator is a tin of liquid acid and Kevin tips it onto him and Jason is gone.

Kevin walks off and tells the police. But the police reckon he's absolutely mad and they put him in therapy for three years. And in Kevin's room a year later, he sees blood running down the wall. But the next moment he looked at it and it was gone.

And that was the story of Jason.

(Extracted from Kevin's story)

Kevin was a haemophiliac, and he was having difficulties in coming to terms with his illness. Kevin liked to provoke fights because everyone would become very alarmed and worry about his safety. Because people had to be so careful about his physical safety, Kevin found he could manipulate them and was, consequently, very uncertain about the limits he or anyone else could put on his behaviour. He did not like having to take care 'like a girl' and made every effort to show how tough he was. His first remarks to me were boasts about how he had seen many videos classified for older audiences. He acted in an autocratic manner, as if he owned the school, and was very dismissive of people's attempts to make him behave. Clearly, Kevin's story powerfully communicates his emotional interests. If fiction writing is serious play, what is Kevin 'playing at' in his story?

If we reconsider Kevin's story in the light of this information, we can see that the murderous hunting of a small and vulnerable boy might relate to some of his fears and fantasies about his dangerous illness. For a boy who is acting out his anxieties about whether the adult world can safely contain his difficult behaviour, the murdering Jason seems unstoppable and powerful. To be able to rehearse these fears in the metaphoric and distanced form of a story enables Kevin to turn what may feel like similarly uncontainable fears (as evidenced in his uncontrollable behaviour) into containable, because symbolised, thoughts.

There are a number of interesting 'containing' aspects to this dictated story. First, language itself contains, fixing inchoate anxieties by giving them a name and a narrative trajectory which can be controlled. Second, writing, by its somewhat paradoxical permanence and its availability to alteration, also offers a way of holding or 'freezing' the events and feelings, where they can be scrutinised and transformed, but can also be 'caught' as in a net and rendered safe. Third, the presence of an adult scribe, controlled by the child–author, but seemingly able to listen to and write down this terrible story without being overwhelmed, gives the child hope that these ideas can be contemplated without panic. In contrast, most adults in real life had to respond with alacrity to Kevin's alarming attempts to court physical harm. Calmly writing down the terrifying events, responding to them in ways that show how these things can be thought about and talked about, is one of the important roles the scribe embodies.

Kevin's approach to dictating was very different from Jay's. Jay had talked amicably to his scribe, and then dictated. Kevin, for whom I was the scribe, launched into a magisterial dictation at a brisk pace with hardly a pause for thought. He did not converse with me at all, but began at once on his thriller, drawing on his knowledge of various video villains to produce Freddie/Jason (the name changes), the murderer who hunts Kevin across continents. It was only after the whole story had been written down, that Kevin was willing to talk about it, and then only after several rapt and silent readings of the text. This process continued over a number of sessions in the same manner. He reproduced accurately the language of the film dialogues, and in the excerpt seems to have been describing a film scene from memory.

At the end of each chapter, he would adopt an American accent (claiming at the same time that he was 'half-American') and switch to the register of the film-trailer, using language to raise suspense and to entice the reader to read the next chapter. 'So, Kevin has gone to Manhattan, has he? If you listen to our story in two weeks' time, you'll never get away then. At least not yet! So, find out in two weeks' time.' Unlike most other children, Kevin did not want or talk about his story, or to chat; and the idea of using this text to teach Kevin about tenses or similes seemed very far from the point. Indeed, it would have been futile, since he was quite unable to take in such lessons. Nevertheless, we can see that, as Kress suggested, even Kevin is making choices regarding what is *criterial* about a story, and this is reflected in his choice of genre and its syntax and vocabulary.

The intersubjective relationship with the scribe, referred to above, seems to be very important to the writing of these emotionally resonant kinds of text. We are already aware of the fundamental importance of relationships with others in order for learning to take place. From infancy onwards, 'for his or her emotional and cognitive development, the baby needs to have experience of, and interaction with, a consistent human caretaker' (Trevarthen *et al.* 1996). Emotional growth, on the one hand, and thinking and learning, on the other, are clearly linked. In the dictated story activity, the child is the author, and the adult for the most part follows the child's play-in-fiction. The adult is thus engaged in the kind of contingent support of the child's meaning that has been identified as a significant feature of early child-rearing, language development and learning (Bruner 1983). Just as carers who are 'tuned into' their infants enable babies to move from a 'presymbolic level of experience to a mature symbolic representational level', so does the story dictated to an adult scribe allow children to make symbolic representations which reflect their most fundamental concerns. In playing out in fictions some of the emotional experiences that trouble them, children can begin to appraise the significance and meaning of those emotional experiences. What is crucially important for the infant is that someone is there not as interpreter but as receiver of the story.

The scribe's role, therefore, can be understood as being present at and facilitating the child's exploration of meaning. Where the scribe, like a reader, gets involved in the meaning of the text – reacting with surprise, disgust or fear, showing curiosity or concern for the victim – as the narrative requires, she shows herself to be empathic to the narrative the composer needs to tell, as well as modelling reader reactions. In the fiction, the child can experience a more mature symbolic representation of feelings or can explore a range of emotional stances, for example, which enable him or her to overcome difficult feelings and memories, not by acting them out, but by turning them into thoughts.

Dictated stories in the classroom

The use of an adult scribe is already a common practice – witness the work of learning-support assistants and parent-helpers. However, scribing is generally seen in a functional sense: a way of getting text down, without much thought being given to the extensive educational and emotional value of the activity. The use of adult scribes requires a fuller understanding of the value of their role; for example, they should be given guidance on appropriate interventions and on non-intervention as a strategy, responding like a reader, and so on. Furthermore, using an adult scribe is quite different from peer-collaborations, including children scribing for each other, since the learning relationship depends, in the adult form, on an expert–novice relationship, while the peer relationship relates far more to Piagetian concepts of cognitive conflict and the communication of alternative views.

Organising the dictation within the classroom

Some children happily dictate in the classroom, with all the activity around them. Other children, and other teachers, prefer the activity to take place in relative peace and quiet. For example, if the class are working quietly it can be distracting for the children, not to say embarrassing for the author, to dictate text with everybody able to listen. There are opportunities for planning for dictated writing to take place within the Literacy Hour and outside it, especially as schools should be finding time for children to practise extended writing. It is important that texts are typed up, and made into book-form for children to use as reading material. Therefore, there are information-communication opportunities for scribing on the wordprocessor and letting the child make alterations, as part of the drafting, editing and proofreading processes. The texts can be used for comprehension, by making clozed versions of extracts or for sentence and word-level work. These activities can be used individually with the author but also as the basis of work with a group, subject to author's consent, of course.

Dictated texts

Children need to feel that their written communications are valued. Where a child is dictating a text that relates to the work-in-progress in the classroom – whether this is a cross-curricular topic or an English task set for the whole class – his or her responses should be given equal value to those made by other children. Texts should be displayed, made into books for other children to read, be talked about and included in classroom discussions of writing, so that children see that they are, in Frank Smith's famous phrase, part of the 'literacy club'. They are already behaving like authors, and their difficulties with literacy, although important and needing to be developed, do not imply that other fundamental aspects of writing are not in place and functioning well. Our responses to the texts are vitally important in convincing children that we take their ideas and communications seriously. This is not the same as an empty and vapid praising of anything they write. It means that we respond to these texts, as we do to others, as serious attempts to communicate with us, and we comment on how effectively they have managed to do this.

Where children like Kevin seem to be using the dictated story to play out important experiences and feelings in their lives, the story needs to be respected even though the content may be disturbing. This is a delicate matter. I did make Kevin's story into a book, but it was just for him – and this was really what he wanted, to go away and read it over and over on his own – and we did not put it into circulation in the classroom. I did also talk to Kevin's mother about his story, so that she was included in how the story was made and why I thought Kevin might have needed to write it.

The use of dictated stories within the primary classroom has much to offer, both in terms of facilitating extended writing for those children who have difficulties as well as increasing motivation for reading. It can be exploited as text from which sentence- and word-level work can be derived, and it enables children to take risks with their language use, which helps them to develop their writing skills in both linguistic and compositional ways. In addition, the use of adult scribes puts children in a learning relationship of novice to expert that has been demonstrated to be an effective way for children to learn new skills. Moreover, where a relationship between children and their scribes is warm and avoids making judgements, some children will use the fictional opportunities to represent matters of deep emotional concern. These fictions are often felt to be very important to the children who write them, for they enable their authors, as all fiction does, to contemplate the meaning of themselves and their worlds in a way that can make those meanings thinkable, and, sometimes, more bearable.

Note

1   All of case studies used in this chapter are genuine, but the children's names have been changed.

References

Appleyard, J. A. (1994) *Becoming a Reader: the Experience of Fiction from Childhood to Adulthood*, Cambridge: Cambridge University Press.

Bruner, J. (1983) *Child's Talk: Learning to Use Language*, Oxford: Oxford University Press.

Frith, U. (1985) 'Beneath the surface of developmental dyslexia', in K. E. Patterson, J. C. Marshall and M. Colthart (eds), *Surface Dyslexia*, London: Erlbaum.

Goswami, U. and Bryant, P. (1990) *Phonological Skills and Learning to Read*, London: Erlbaum.

Kress, G. (1997) *Before Writing: Rethinking the Paths to Literacy*, London: Routledge.

Meek, M. (1982) *Learning to Read*, London: Bodley Head.

Rosen, M. (1989) *Did I Hear You Write?*, London: André Deutsch.

Smith, B. (1994) *Through Writing to Reading*, London: Routledge.

Steedman, C. (1982) *The Tidy House*, London: Virago Press.

Trevarthen, C., Aitken, K., Papoudi, D. and Robarts, J. (1996) *Children with Autism: Diagnosis and Interventions to Meet Their Needs*, London: Jessica Kingsley Publishers.

Chapter 11

Telling facts

Contrasting voices in recent information books for children

Frances Smith

Young readers (and their parents and teachers) now have an increasingly wide range of information books to choose from, many with such unlikely but inviting titles as *Dinosaurs Divorce* (Brown and Brown 1996) and *The Beginner's Guide to Animal Autopsy* (Parker 1997) – rather a disappointment, this last, on closer inspection. There are, however, many information books which promise more familiar contents. *Tudor Times* (Shuter, Hook and Maguire 1995) is a title which holds no secrets, dealing unsurprisingly with such familiar topics as town and country life, as well as historical events of the period. It has the structure and layout you would expect. The authors present information in the text in a straightforward and unsensational manner; they do not address the reader directly, exaggerate, make jokes or mock other writers, teachers or adults.

A book such as this sets out to provide information, and categorising it as non-fiction does not cause us too many difficulties. We all know, however, that information giving is not confined to volumes on the special shelves or accessed via catalogue numbers: fiction, too, can give us information and tell us truths. In the course of Eloise McGraw's story *The Golden Goblet* (1968), we find out what it was like to to be an apprentice in ancient Egypt: we get to know about houses and food, the significance of the great river, the festivals – and also about cruelties, incidental and institutionalised. The same book, however, tells us deeper truths: what it feels like to be disregarded, the value of friendship, the unhappiness arising from unfulfilled abilities, difficulties inherent in deciding the right course of action. As Margaret Meek (1996) pointed out in *Information and Book Learning*, children find facts in both fiction and non-fiction. She shows us the errors involved in supposing that non-fiction books are the sole source of information, that narratives are always stories and stories always fictive.

It is difficult to disagree with Meek's conviction that problematic issues, moral attitudes and understandings are most effectively presented in novels and picture-books. All are explored in Anne Fine's novel *Goggle-Eyes* in which a girl comes to some resolution of her feelings about her divorced mother's new relationship through helping a friend in a similar situation. The story is threaded through by Kitty's realistic, and often funny, evaluation of her feelings and how they come to change. Towards the end, we are invited, through the words of Kitty's teacher, to reflect on what books can do for their readers:

> Living your life is a long and doggy business, says Mrs Lupey. And stories and books help. Some help you with the living itself. Some help you just take a break. The best do both at the same time.
>
> (Fine 1990: 139)

Some recent series of information books for children aim to fulfil Mrs Lupey's last category. I want to look closely at a few of those which deal with historical topics, in order to reflect on some of the issues that arise when we look below the surface of what is reported and try to disentangle some of the different voices that are involved in the telling. Mikhail Bakhtin, the Russian critic and theorist, used the term 'change of speaking subjects' for the way voices, ideas and languages respond to and conflict with each other in texts (Bakhtin 1993: 81).[1] What kinds of speaking subject are telling us facts in these texts? Do the voices combine to tell the same tale, or are there tensions between the different perspectives? What might children understand of all this? I draw on some insights from a group of 11-year-old readers[2] to consider children's understanding of different ways of telling in these books.

There have always been children's books that live in the borderline area between fact and fiction. There are books that come from a long and distinguished tradition of historical fiction, such as *The Golden Goblet* described above, in which we have a clear narrative structure with the satisfying resolution you would expect in a children's novel. Readers accept McGraw's story as fiction and assume that the details of everyday life are based on fact. The jacket is clear about the book's aims, claiming it will be enjoyed 'not only for its suspense and fast-moving action but for its fascinating and authentic picture of daily life in Egypt'. Both author and reader know what is expected of them in books like this: from their respective vantage points, each will see the story as fiction, but not fantasy: it *could* have happened.

At the factual (or at least ideational) end of the continuum, there are books which use fiction to express facts, concepts or ideas. These books also have a long history and reflect many branches of knowledge. Fifty years ago in *Out with Romany by Meadow and Stream* (Bramwell Evens 1942) the conversations between the narrator, Romany, and his young friend provided the inquiring child reader with an understanding of the habits of owls and voles; today young readers can find out about philosophy from *Sophie's World* (Gaarder 1995) or relativity from *The Cosmic Professor* (Donkin 1997). Often these books include a fictional child character with whom the young reader can identify; this fictional child is a device found even in books which present themselves as biographies.

Then there are books which use non-fiction genres such as diaries or magazine formats to present fictional matters. *The Dinosaur's Book of Dinosaurs* (Brumpton 1990) is a complex example. It is neither a story nor a factual report, but seemingly a book written by a young dinosaur, Roger. To a greater degree than in either of the previous books, fiction and fact are interwoven throughout this one. It looks like a picture-book fiction: the dinosaurs it depicts watch television, go on holidays and play in football teams. It does, however, introduce historically accurate information among the anachronisms, and it has many conventional non-fiction structural features. My 11-year-olds were delighted with it: they appreciated the visual–verbal punning (such as a palm tree labelled 'my family tree') and showed immediate understanding of its mix of factual and fictional elements.

In Mrs Lupey's terms, *The Dinosaur's Book* helps you 'take a break', and it does this in ways that distinguish it markedly from the previous two books. One such way is through affectionate parody – of the 'topic' books children write and of the many other genres included in the book: photo albums, pictorial maps, questionnaires, team lists, riddles, recipes, teenage romance pages. At another level, it entertains through the reader's complicity with the writer in pretending something is true when it is not. In the Preface the author explains that the text was posted to him, written in a school exercise-book. The opening sentence is: 'At long last, here is a dinosaur book written *by* a dinosaur!' At once, comfortable conventions about the respective roles of writer and reader are called into question. And, unlike the writers of the previous books, this writer is indubitably there for the reader (the narrator, Roger, also takes an active role in addressing the reader, continually interrupting the text with a running commentary, postscripts and joky comments).

This book, then, is unlike the previous cases of borderline genre in important ways. It incorporates self-conscious reference to its own making. It complicates the relationship between teller and told and clouds the distinction between author and narrator. Readers know that books like this one are not what they say they are, even when the author vouches for their authenticity.

Such texts undoubtedly relate factual matter; but their use of fiction is more complicated. *The Golden Goblet* exemplifies what we normally think of as fiction: imaginative storytelling, more specifically in the form of a prose narrative, for example the novel or the short story. 'Fiction' also has other meanings, however. In everyday conversation, fiction can mean something made up – as in the invented dialogues between expert and child in fictionalised biographies – or even something deceptive, and both these meanings clearly apply to large parts of *The Dinosaur's Book of Dinosaurs*.

Fiction, in all these senses, is powerful. It can present alternatives to reality; it can play with what is possible and it can assert what is not (but might be). These possibilities are prominent in some recent children's information books. Although they are classed as non-fiction, they have fictional narrators, fake documents and invented autobiographies which challenge existing expectations of the non-fiction genre. The history books among them have titles such as *What They Don't Tell You About World War II* (Fowke 1997), *Truly Terrible Tales* (Marlowe 1997) and *The Blitzed Brits* (Deary 1994). A brief glance shows how these books differ from traditional children's non-fiction. The authors relish alliteration and wordplay and present a joky image of their contents. *The Blitzed Brits*, for example, has a cartoon picture on its cover of a 1940s family in gas masks, standing amid the ruin of their bombed house; a speech bubble has one parent ask 'Do you think we'll need to redecorate, darling?'

What lies behind these confident and noisy exteriors? Some of the books which cover the same field as *Tudor Times*, the traditional information book described earlier, are clearly at the fictional end of the continuum: *The Lost Diary of Henry VIII's Executioner* (Barlow and Skidmore 1997) claims to contain the diaries and scrapbook cuttings of Watkyn 'Chopper' Smith, found by the authors during building work on a cottage; others are closer in their intention to traditional history books, despite titles like *Plotting and Chopping* (Anderson 1995). The main body of this chapter focuses on two of these: *The Terrible Tudors* (Deary and Tonge 1993) and *History in a Hurry: Tudors* (Farman 1997); reference will also be made to several of the titles already mentioned.

These two books are explicit about what they are trying to do – namely provide information about the Tudors in ways that will entertain readers who find conventional history books boring. *Terrible Tudors* (hereafter *TT* in citations) includes puzzles, quizzes and activities in the text; it promises to reveal 'the sort of facts that teachers never bother to tell you' (*TT*: 8). It aims to concentrate, not on kings and dates, but on ordinary people, their feelings and experiences: 'what made them laugh and cry, what made them suffer and die'. There are extracts from original sources in this book; and readers are sometimes encouraged to act as historians themselves and to make their own judgements about such sources.

History in a Hurry (HH) has no activities or sources, is considerably more flippant in tone and has a limited remit: 'All you need to know (and a little bit less) about the Tudors' (back cover). It makes clear its aim – to be 'very good, very short, very funny (and very cheap)', – and at £1.99 it certainly is the latter. A major feature is the running dialogue, conducted in the text and in footnotes, between the writer figure and his editor.

Such aims mark a departure not only from traditional information books, but also from the other kinds of books on the borderline between fact and fiction. While in some respects these books are similar to traditional history books – in the selection of kings and queens, life in town and country, health and sickness as factual information, and in the use of trivia and exotica as interesting facts – there is a greater emphasis on the gruesome details of illnesses, executions and torture and a more profound departure from the norm in their presentation of facts, within a fictional framework.

I discussed this with my four 11-year-old readers. They talked about what was likely to be factual and what invented in these books, showing an increasing understanding, as they spoke, of the hybrid nature of these books and the variety of forms they took. They contrasted books such as *Terrible Tudors* ('mostly fact') with *Lost Diary* ('mostly joke'). They tried to identify degrees of truth, drawing on their knowledge of other books, including *The Diary of Anne Frank*. They returned several times to the idea that 'fact' is not a simple concept: it can underpin fiction to differing extents, for example in the use of historical events in *Lost Diary* or in the general truths about adolescence which inform Adrian Mole's diary; it may be transmitted in different ways, for example as diary, narration or summary; it can be adapted, extended or edited.

They also commented on how they read these books, moving the focus to a consideration of genre. One child noted that such books are not like an extended narrative or factual account: 'You can open it anywhere and read – not the kind you need to start at the beginning and put your bookmark in.' Another pointed to the 'cartoony' illustrations, saying that they indicated the 'kind of book you have to read for yourself, not [have it] read to [you], because of the pictures'. It was 'not like reading a fact book, not like reading a cartoon', but 'what you're reading is real'. In addition, the children recognised fiction in these books, both in the sense of embedded stories and in its second meaning of something made up or deceptive.

The main way in which these books differ from traditional tellings is in the prominence given to the narrator as a speaking subject. The writer does not maintain a conventional academic distance from his subject and readers, but appears in the role of a fictional narrator, with a character and opinions of his own. The following extracts dealing with Shakespeare provide a useful comparison of traditional and non-traditional approaches, starting with the traditional history book *Tudor Times*, followed by the less conventional *Terrible Tudors*.

> William Shakespeare acted and wrote plays in the reigns of Elizabeth I and James I. He was very popular at the time and many of his plays are still performed today.
>
> (Shuter, Hook and Maguire 1995: 34)

> Terrible Shakespeare has been torturing school pupils for hundreds of years!
>
> It isn't his fault, though. Teachers were taught by teachers who were taught, 'Shakespeare is the greatest poet and playwright ever. You are

going to listen to him even if it bores the knickers off you! Now sit still and stop yawning!'

In fact, Shakespeare didn't write for school pupils to read his plays and study every last word. He wrote the plays to be *acted* and *enjoyed* . . . so *act* them and *enjoy* them!

(*TT*: 52; emphases in original)

Shakespeare is not mentioned at all in the chapter on Tudor theatre in *History in a Hurry: Tudors*, which leads to a sarcastic intervention by the 'fussy editor, Susie' in a footnote: 'Don't you think that in a chapter on Entertainment in Elizabethan times that we should just maybe mention the most famous playwright ever? (Ed.)', and the terse rejoinder from the author 'No (JF)' (*HH*: 24).

In the traditional telling, facts are stated without comment. Information is given in an authoritative and apparently impartial way, but is lacking in specificity; its simplification give it a curiously understated tone. In *Terrible Tudors* and *History in a Hurry*, there is a quite different relationship between teller and told, indeed there are different tellers altogether: the writers actually take part in the telling as developed fictional characters, in a more pronounced way than do Keith and Roger in *The Dinosaur's Book of Dinosaurs*. They talk directly to us in the first person – indeed at times they harangue us – and make no attempt to be impartial.

What we have in these books are writers creating a fictional character for themselves, similar to the role of a first-person narrator in fiction. The male narrator in *Terrible Tudors* is down to earth, dismissive of adult and teacher authority – 'parents, grandparents, teachers and other old fogeys' (*TT*: 26) – and stresses his ordinariness: the book is for 'People like you and me. Commoners! (Well, I'm dead common, I don't know about you!)' (ibid.: 8).

The narrator in *History in a Hurry* is more laddish in his mode of talking, telling us that Henry VIII's eighteenth birthday celebrations beat his own 'Boots gift token and free half at the Dog and Dungheap' (*HH*: 8). Through the quarrels and insults which permeate the text and footnotes of this book, the (male) narrator is presented as joky, slipshod, lacking in historical knowledge, but likeable, while his fictional (female) editor is long-suffering, but humourless, pedantic, sarcastic – and educated. The overwhelming opinion of the class I interviewed was that these kinds of book are the preserve of male writers. Male voices are seen to be doing the telling here (and allocating the roles?).

Most adult readers understand the-writer-in-the-text as a device, a construct. My group had not thought much about who was doing the telling before we talked, but, presented with these books and a range of other first-person narratives, they developed a lively discussion about the author–narrator relationship.

They saw some first-person narrators, in stories they knew and in *Lost Diary*, as clearly fictional like Roger Dinosaur – 'a made-up personality'. They were by no means so sure about other books, however. They did not seem to see the first-person narrator of *Terrible Tudors* as expressing views in any way different from those of the actual author, but after some discussion decided that the real John Farman, author of *History in a Hurry*, was not the uninformed writer presented in the text. The narrator of the fictionalised biography of Albert Einstein (Donkin 1997), who recounts a boyhood adventure when he met Einstein, created the most doubt – they concluded that he could be relating an actual event.

The fictional narrator in all these history books is a dominant voice, overtly selecting and shaping information. In *Terrible Tudors*, he does more: he shapes a response to history as a subject, promoting an investigative approach and encouraging pupil opinion in its use of evidence, questions and comment. He also attacks other ways in which history is told:

> A 1980 school history book said. . . . *All in all the Elizabethan Age was an extremely exciting time to be alive.* But this is a *Horrible History* book. You make up your own mind about how 'exciting' it was when you have the real facts.
>
> (*TT*: 20)

The approach to history in these newer books has its advantages. Many of the young readers I asked claimed to have enjoyed the books, particularly boys, and were able to explain why. They are 'giving you information and making you laugh', one child told me. Among those who liked these books 'a lot' or 'very much indeed' in the class I surveyed, most made favourable mention of information as well as humour. These books appear to challenge ways of thinking about the provision of information, who can tell it and who is being told. Readers can learn that there may be different views on which facts are important, and that there is more than one way to present them. Some books show children that historical conclusions must be tentative and based on the evidence available; that more than one interpretation is possible. They may learn that history can be enjoyed by everyone, and that everyone can have an opinion, not only the experts.

Beneath the confident voice of the tellers in these books, however, there are other voices, other perspectives, speaking to us and to each other. Sometimes these voices conflict with one another; there are tensions, ambivalences and silences.

'Giving you information' does not always sit comfortably with 'making you laugh'. In some of these books, a tension is evident when the narrator seems to take on alternate roles as instructor and entertainer. The narrator of *Terrible Tudors* makes us laugh, but also speaks to us in didactic fashion: 'Remember, history is not always simple or straightforward' (*TT*: 63). He interrupts his instructions for using a Stanley knife to make a quill pen to remind readers that they need an adult 'to make sure you don't get chopped fingers on the table!' The sudden usefulness of adults after the derision that has previously been heaped on them is understandable, but perhaps symptomatic of a deeper ambivalence between the voices of instructor and entertainer in this book. These books have to inform their readers as well as amuse them; they cannot assume that their readers already know all the history so that they can merely satirise it, as the authors could in *1066 And All That* (Sellars and Yeatman 1930).

We have in this dual voice of instructor–entertainer an example of dialogism, the double-voiced discourse which Bakhtin identified in novels and popular speech when differing intentions are expressed: 'the direct intention of the character who is speaking, and the refracted intention of the author' (Bakhtin 1981: 324). The intention of the authors – to prevent an accident with a Stanley knife – is mediated through the breezy voice of his fictional narrator, whose exaggeration and humorous exclamation in fact serves to lessen the impact of the warning.

As Sue Vice (1997: 45) points out, Bakhtin used the term 'dialogism' both for particular instances of language such as this, where two distinct voices exist in one utterance, and more widely as a defining property of language itself. Both senses are evident in these books. We have already seen the former in the shifting role of the narrator, and it is evident also in the way readers can become a voice in the dialogue through their imagined response – 'the consciousness of the listener . . . pregnant with responses and objections' (Bakhtin 1981: 281). In *Terrible Tudors*, the narrator mocks the medicinal use of herbs, then has to recognise the reader's reasonable objection that these are used today – but he dismisses this as irrelevant: but would you take one from a Tudor apothecary who didn't know the importance of washing their hands before handling your medicine?' (*TT*: 22).

Double-voicedness is evident also in the self-consciousness of the books, their readiness to talk to themselves, to reflect on their own making, within the narration – 'Is this getting boring? I think I'll stop here' (*HH*: 40) – and it is discernible in the elaborate framing devices setting up the supposed diary in *Lost Diary*.

Bakhtin's second sense of dialogism is evident in settings where no words are neutral:

All words have the taste of a profession, a genre, a tendency, a party, a particular work, a particular person, a generation, an age group, the day and hour. Every word tastes of the context and contexts in which it has lived its intense social life; all words and all forms are inhabited by intentions.

(Bakhtin 1981: 293)

We see this in the use of the word 'facts' in these books; the serious meanings this word brings with it from past uses – data, information, reports – contrast with its uses in these books: hidden facts, 'interesting' facts, exotica. These conflicting uses of a word result at times in conscious self-parody. There are recurring sections in *History in a Hurry* with titles such as 'Useless Facts No. 28' (*HH*: 29), a clear reference to sections in other information books with the same kind of trivia. These facts are seemingly mocked here by the title, but are simultaneously valued for their interest.

This dialogic ambivalence between instruction and entertainment is seen, too, in a struggle between the characteristic voice of the historian and the jocularity of the entertainer's interjections. We see formal historical writing in the abstractions, subject-specific vocabulary and nominalisations appropriate to this genre. Mary tries 'to return England to the Catholic faith' (*TT*: 18), there is 'a gradual shift from wheat growing to the less labour intensive sheep-rearing' (*HH*: 27). These are 'another's speech in another's language' (Bakhtin 1981: 324). What we encounter, however, is not only the representation of the genre, but a response to its language and voice, a refashioning of another's words in one's own language, as Bakhtin described it. Convoluted explanations of genealogy in the more formal history books are satirised: 'When Henry VII died, Henry Jnr, the King's old youngest son, but now the King's new oldest son because the old oldest son had popped his clogs' (*HH*: 8). So, too, is their vocabulary, as when we read of a 'child of an unlawful onion' (ibid.: 21) (the joke is explained in a footnote).

Another language speaking to us in these texts besides the language of different written genres is spoken language itself: the hesitations and interruptions; the asides – 'Personally, I would have made a bog-awful hero. I'd tell anyone *anything* at the threat of a little light tickling' (*HH*: 47); the colloquial usages – 'Get it? Oh, never mind' (*TT*: 54); the truncated sentences and shared references. All of these are typical of the representation of informal spoken language in writing.

This version of spoken language, seen particularly in remarks addressed directly to the reader, often shades into another language, that of popular journalism. This is sometimes overt, as in *Lost Diary* where there is a succession of extracts from front pages of 'Ye Sonne. England's favourite dailey. Still only five groats' (Barlow and Skidmore 1997: 11). The language of tabloids is seen also in the prevalence of such language play as alliteration and punning. As Guy Cook shows us, in a fascinating study of songs, graffiti, puns and popular journalism, sometimes this delight in inventiveness raises questions:

> [T]he tabloid combination of linguistic inventiveness and dexterity with banal subject matter or objectionable opinion highlights the degree to

which clever form should serve content, and the degree to which form may even become content.

(Cook 1996: 217)

Cook goes on to propose that language play can actually *create* as well as reflect the levity or seriousness of a news item. We can see something similar in these books in a tension between the roles of instructor and entertainer which involves a silence – about the values and understandings we can take from history. Cruelty is often reported in the same light-hearted way as are Tudor table manners. One of the activities in *Terrible Tudors* involves matching cartoon figures of criminals with sketches of the appropriate punishments, such as burning alive and branding. In *Lost Diary*, 'Chopper' Smith mentions in passing the burning of fourteen heretics, adding merely 'Religion! It's a complicated game' (Barlow and Skidmore 1997: 74). In *History in a Hurry*, we read that

> Queen Elizabeth was not averse to a bit of torture, and when Robert Holt, a priest, was 'racked' and then hung, the crowd noticed that he was mysteriously without fingernails (ouch times ten). It had all been on her recommendation (or should I say rackommendation?).
>
> (HH: 47)

The chatty tone – 'a bit of torture' – the asides in parentheses and the final pun invite readers to laugh, but the facts do not. The fictional narrator's voice seems to be pulling against the voice of the factual information being presented to us. These are features of adult satiric writing, of course, from Swift's *A Modest Proposal* onwards and we know that children have always relished laughing at taboo topics. I wondered, therefore, how the children in my group would regard this tension between content and presentation.

The children were pragmatic when we discussed this. 'They're only joking to make it more interesting', and 'It happened a long time ago', were typical responses. It was only when I probed a little further that they identified some things they might not joke about: concentration camps, 'because it would offend Jews'; and God, 'because [the books have] got to sell – you don't know who's going to be reading [them]'. The relation of horrors in a detached, flippant or ironic manner is a marked feature of these books. Child readers may not, though, bring enough prior understanding of the meaning of these events to contribute to – or read against – an ironic intention. Is this reading in fact being imposed on them? Young readers may well be distanced from all but superficial understandings of the events of the past, when it is the way in which the past is told that appears to matter rather than what is told. The effect is to smooth out the relative significance of different facts and events, so that beheadings (or worse) are on a par with remedies for toothache, and both are equally funny. We should note that the earliest of the three books, *Terrible Tudors*, is somewhat different here. It has its share of the gruesome but is clearer about its aim – to 'amaze you and teach you and amuse you, and sometimes make you sad' (*TT*: 8). It includes stories which engage the reader's feelings: for instance, there is a moving narrative account of the death of Margaret Clitheroe, an ordinary woman who died for her religious beliefs. The two later books, both published in 1997, emphasise amazement and amusement rather than learning or empathy, and only infrequently seem to invoke an affective dimension.

One young reader provided me with a different perspective on these books. He compared them with *Coping with Teachers* (Corey 1991), one of several light-hearted books giving spoof advice on personal problems. Should these two books be seen in the same light, as books which help you 'take a break'? I'm not sure. Corey's book can assume children's prior knowledge of the content (teachers, parents, their peers) as a basis for humour; but when books deal with a historical period, there may be other implications.

Coping with Teachers presents itself as a challenge to authority. The books I have discussed share this approach to different degrees, disputing what history might be, who is qualified to write about it and how it should be read. Accepted norms and taboos are flouted, as also is reverence for authority figures. It seems to me, however, that while there seem to be elements of subversion in these books, any real challenge to established ways of thinking about history is safely contained. There is, for example, little attempt to question the present by relating it to the past, and humour is often used to deflect thought, rather than to promote it: 'Funny thing, progress, it always seems to be the poor that pay for it. Ah well, c'est la vie' (*HH*: 7).

So, although these books signal an apparently expansive impetus – towards diversity and anarchy – there are stronger forces containing thinking within conventional modes and commercial necessities. Purchase looms large at the end of the books, in invitations to buy more, and some children recognised this: as one of my readers noted of a provocative blurb: 'He's only kidding. He wants you to read it.' The books are basically conservative and comfortably nasty – the authority figures they challenge are caricatures. The final word of *Terrible Tudors* is that things are all right nowadays.

So we have different voices and perspectives overlapping each other, sometimes conflicting with each other and sometimes existing side by side in an ambivalent fashion. For the children we teach, it may be less important to try to come to a consensus about the propriety of this kind of approach to history (or to humour) in writing aimed at children than to provide opportunities for young readers to become aware of these voices, to discuss what different books are for, their underlying values and children's own responses to them.

Margaret Meek speaks of the value to children's intellectual growth of a 'collaborative focus on a task with an adult as well as a book' (Meek

1996: 97). My readers certainly extended my existing ideas about the value of adults and children working together; they also gave me new things to think about. On the basis of this collaboration and the insights to which it gave rise, I end this chapter with five questions which perhaps will inform collaborative reading of these and other information books. Of any such book, the following questions might usefully be asked:

1   How is this text true? We can encourage children to discuss fact, invention and make-believe, and even perhaps something of the problematic nature of 'truth'. We can help them to understand that facts are chosen, can be presented in different ways in different genres, can be adapted and extended – and that there are different kinds of truth, factual and imaginative.

2   Who is saying this – who is presenting the facts or proposing the values? As they develop as readers, children can be helped to consider the different voices speaking in texts (and their agendas). They can look at the writer's presence in both fiction and information books and the special case of first-person narration.

3   What do you think of the writer's views? What can be seen as valid humour? How far a distance in time is required to allow a comic approach to historical events, or are there values that remain inappropriate objects of humour? Children can consider what may not be funny – and to whom – values, assumptions, censorship, tolerance. Beginning insights, such as have been seen from the children here, can be developed further in different contexts.

4   Why is it like this – why has the writer chosen this structure and layout, these sentences and words? We can encourage children to think more about the purposes, literary and otherwise, that underlie texts and how these are expressed at text and sentence levels. My group, for example, was aware that writers have reasons for the choices they make and that books are not independent of other forces, including market ones.

5   How is it like other books? How does the text relate to others in the same genre (or to those dealing with the same topic in other genres)? How far does it use intertextual devices – references to other books or the meanings accrued to words in other texts? As with the previous question, this is one that my readers taught me, as they referred to a wide variety of other reading, from the *Beano* to *The Diary of Anne Frank*, in their discussions of matters such as verbal–visual links in different genres, first-person narration and ways of reading. My group was also aware of ways in which these books draw on other texts. Not all references, however, were open to them – they did not have the background knowledge to relate 'Gotcha!' in a parody of the *Sun* to the notorious headline used in the Falklands War.

These are questions, perhaps, which are not easy to answer, but which may help our young readers towards critical reading and a deeper understanding of what is involved when levity and seriousness meet. Perhaps the most important lesson they can learn is that sometimes it is worth looking below the surface of what they are reading and that it is always worth talking about their reading with other people.

Notes

1 My references to Bakhtin's thinking have drawn on the insights of Sue Vice in *Introducing Bakhtin* (1997) and Rob Pope in *The English Studies' Book* (1998).
2 I owe thanks to Hilary Hladky and her year 6 class at Milton Road Junior School, Cambridge, for their help with this chapter, and in particular to the four children whose discussion was recorded.

References

Anderson, S. (1995) *Plotting and Chopping*, Harmondsworth: Penguin.

Bakhtin, M. (1968) *Rabelais and His World*, trans. H. Iwolsky, Cambridge, MA: MIT Press.

—— (1981) 'Discourse in the novel', in M. Holquist (ed.), *The Dialogical Imagination*, trans. C. Emerson and M. Holquist, Austin, TX: University of Texas Press.

—— (1993) 'The problem of speech genres', in C. Emerson and M. Holquist (eds), *Speech Genres and Other Late Essays*, trans. V. McGee, Austin, TX: University of Texas Press.

Barlow, S. and Skidmore, S. (1997) *The Lost Diary of Henry VIII's Executioner*, London: Collins.

Bramwell Evens, G. (1942) *Out with Romany by Meadow and Stream*, Bickley, Kent: University of London Press.

Brown, L. K. and Brown, M. (1996) *Dinosaurs Divorce*, Glasgow: Collins.

Brumpton, K. (1990) *The Dinosaur's Book of Dinosaurs*, London: Orchard Books.

Cook, G. (1996) 'Language play in English', in Janet Maybin and Neil Mercer (eds.), *Using English: From Conversation to Canon*, London: Routledge.

Corey, P. (1981) *Coping with Teachers*, London: Scholastic.

Deary, T. (1994) *The Blitzed Brits*, London: Scholastic.

Deary, T. and Tonge, N. (1993) *The Terrible Tudors*, London: Scholastic.

Donkin, A. (1997) *The Cosmic Professor*, Hove: Macdonald.

Farman, J. (1997) *History in a Hurry: Tudors*, London: Macmillan.

Fine, A. (1990) *Goggle-Eyes*, Harmondsworth: Penguin Books.

Fowke, B. (1997) *What They Don't Tell You About World War II*, Sevenoaks: Hodder & Stoughton.

Gaarder, J. (1995) *Sophie's World*, London: Phoenix.

Marlowe, J. (1997) *Truly Terrible Tales: Explorers*, London: Hodder & Stoughton.

McGraw, E. J. (1968) *The Golden Goblet*, Harmondsworth: Penguin.

Meek, M. (1996) *Information and Book Learning*, Woodchester: Thimble Press.

Parker, S. (1997) *The Beginner's Guide to Animal Autopsy*, London: Aladdin/Watts.

Pope, R. (1998) *The English Studies' Book*, London: Routledge.

Sellars, W. and Yeatman, R. (1930) *1066 And All That*, London: Methuen.

Shuter, J., Hook, A. and Maguire, J. (1995) *Tudor Times*, Oxford: Heinemann.

Vice, S. (1997) *Introducing Bakhtin*, Manchester: Manchester University Press.

Chapter 12

Anne Fine's stories for life

Jim Jones

> Living your life is a long and doggy business. . . . And stories and books help. Some help you with the living itself. Some help you just take a break. The best do both at the same time.
>
> (*Goggle-Eyes*: 139)

This is Anne Fine talking. It is not Anne Fine 'straight', of course; it is the voice of Kitty, the narrator of *Goggle-Eyes*, and she is telling us what good stories are for. Kitty is quoting her teacher, so we are already at two steps' remove from Anne Fine herself; and the teacher's name is Mrs Lupey – '*Loopy*' to the teenage girls in her charge: another layer of disguise. If it is messages you are looking for, they are not going to be handed you on a plate.

So how do we know that this is Anne Fine's voice? Because her novels tell us. Two strands – threads, strings, *ropes* – run through her work, and they are the two that Kitty has latched on to.

First, her novels help you take a break, leading you into a world where the everyday is often given a fantastical spin. A divorced father is missing his children? Get him to dress up as a middle-aged woman to be his ex-wife's housekeeper and childminder (*Madame Doubtfire*). A bully is terrorising some of the pupils in his primary class? Get an angel to join the school to come and sort it out (*The Angel of Nitshill Road*). A boy, like everyone in his school, takes gender roles for granted? Turn him into a girl for a day (*Bill's New Frock*). These novels are *entertainments*. They do what novels should do: help you take a break from your ordinary life – often into quite bizarre realms. (It is hardly surprising that film producers have cottoned on to their potential.)

But they always keep at least one foot firmly on the ground. And that is how they do the second thing that Kitty – or Mrs Lupey, or Anne Fine – celebrates: they help you with the living itself. This is the clever bit. Even if her novels allow the anchor to loosen a little (to switch metaphors mid-stream, as it were), it never slips entirely. The novels already mentioned are fixed into the realities of school or family life, and Anne Fine does this well.

In fact, only a few of her novels are based on an entirely fantastical premiss. Most of her work is about the realities of everyday life as experienced by children. Younger readers will encounter characters who are afraid of the dark (*The Haunting of Pip Parker*), who are learning about not talking to strangers (*Stranger Danger?*), or who want to keep a pet in a cage (*Countdown*). Older readers have to cover tougher ground: the effect on family life of a relative with Alzheimer's (*The Granny Project*) or of a divorce (*Madame Doubtfire*); and – a rich seam, this – the intrusiveness of a divorced parent's new spouse (*Goggle-Eyes, Step by Wicked Step*).

The perils of family life, growing up, school – whatever – are always real in Anne Fine's novels, and this goes for the fantasies as well as her more realistic books. Mind you, even 'realistic' is a slippery term when one is dealing with this author: she is just as playful with the narrative in these novels, just as willing to head off in unexpected directions, as she is in the fantasies. Anne Fine is always playing games, but they are serious games, taking the reader's perceptions to places they are not used to visiting. Just as all her novels are real, so they are all *jeux d'esprit*. There is a lot to be gained from studying them, a lot for teachers and pupils to work with.

Some help you with the living itself

Anne Fine made her reputation with the novels she wrote for older readers. It is not surprising that these tread difficult ground. But over the past ten years or so she has written also for a younger readership. One publisher, Puffin, divides her output into three categories: for younger, 'middle-range' and older readers. This is helpful – but it should not prevent us from seeing that, whatever the intended audience, Anne Fine is emphatically the same writer. Her novels are all embedded in the familiar and, whatever their focus, all embrace the wider theme of personal growth – of learning through (often difficult) experience.

Family life

The most important relationships in any child's life are those that develop in the family home. These relationships in Anne Fine's novels are rich, entertaining – and the bringers of almost unimaginable stress. Things are bad enough when the family holds together: the 'banshee' in *The Book of the Banshee* (1991) is the narrator's sister, transformed by puberty into a shrieking monster. In *The Granny Project* (1983), the question of what to do about the continuing presence of the children's increasingly senile relative leads to a state, almost, of guerrilla warfare between them and their parents.

It is when things break up – or, worse, when single parents find a new partner – that the fun really starts. *Madame Doubtfire* (1987), Anne Fine's most famous novel, is not mere farce, even though its farcical elements are highly entertaining, in both the original version and in the film starring Robin Williams. That novel is really about *love*: Daniel goes to outrageous lengths because he cannot bear to be separated from his children.

In *Goggle-Eyes* Kitty, the book's narrator, is chosen by her teacher to help sort out another girl's problem: Helly is in floods of tears because, as Kitty guesses with only a few clues, '"Your mum's going to marry that man with grey hair! . . . And you think he's a proper creep! You've thought he was a creep all along . . ."' (p. 13). This is Chapter 1, and Helly confirms that she cannot stand 'Toad Shoes'. The rest of the novel consists, however, not of Helly's story but of Kitty's. Goggle-Eyes is the new man in Kitty's mother's life and – as her nickname for him suggests – Kitty wishes he was not. Or, she *used* to: 123 pages after beginning her story, and many months after first meeting Goggle-Eyes, she admits: '"I honestly believe, if he and Mum got married, I wouldn't mind"' (p. 138). Her story works its miracle on the previously distraught Helly. She leaves, smiling, and this is where Kitty's hymn of praise to the power of story comes in.

At one level, the message is almost too simple: time is a great healer. But Anne Fine's novels are always more interesting than that. Kitty knows that her opinions have changed because she has been able to reflect on her own growing understanding of the adults in her life. Mrs Lupey knew all about Goggle-Eyes because Kitty has written page after page about him in English assignments. Now, Kitty can see how the effect of the new relationship on her mother's happiness has enriched the life of the whole family.

(Anne Fine does not even stop there: Kitty is astute enough to recognise another adult's motives, too. Early on in the novel, she tries to work out why *she* is delegated to comfort Helly, not one of her own friends: 'Helly and I must have *something* in common. . . . "I know!" I cried. "I know why you're so upset!"' (p. 13). And she begins her tale as a sort of gesture of solidarity. At the end of it, she is sure she detects a conspiratorial wink from Mrs Lupey. As the teacher says, 'She spins a good yarn'; and we already know her views on the therapeutic powers of storytelling. But more of that later.)

The later novel *Step by Wicked Step* (1995), also for older readers, takes the themes of step-parents and storytelling even further. At first, we are thrown off the scent: the title, the eerie cover illustration and the opening chapter lead the reader to expect a chiller: 'Even before they reached the haunted house, the night had turned wild . . .' (p. 1). This is all a tease. Anne Fine is playing with her readers' understanding of genre, because in fact the novel is about something else. On a school trip, several characters are thrown together through a combination of unexpectedly foul weather (was it *just* a tease?) and an administrative blip. The only thing the characters in *Step by Wicked Step* have in common is that each is living with a natural parent and a step-parent. They all end up telling their stories, and between them they come to some uncomfortable realisations about the quick solutions some of them had formulated. Colin is a case in point:

> 'He plans to *disappear*.'
> 'I understand how he feels. But he can't do that.'
> 'Why can't I?' asked Colin sullenly.
> 'Because, like Richard Harwick said, you'd just be piling one wrong on to another, till everything was broken from the strain. . . .'
>
> (pp. 132–3)

Richard Harwick had been an inhabitant of the 'haunted house'. They have found his diary, which catalogues the misery that followed his 'disappearance' once his dislike of his stepfather had become unbearable. This is Anne Fine working her narrative on more than one level. All the characters in *Step by Wicked Step* learn something about themselves, and about adult life, by telling their stories and listening to those of other people. The diary is the icing on the cake, rounding off her theme and bringing Colin face to face with his own responsibilities.

So, there *is* family life, and there *is* growth. In each of Anne Fine's family tales, at least one of the characters comes to an important realisation. In the novels which are concerned with step-parents, the children's recognition of the reality of their parents' needs is parallelled in *Madame Doubtfire* by a different recognition: at the end of the novel Daniel's wife realises that his love for their children, and his need for contact with them, are as great as her own. In *The Granny Project*, the children conspire to keep their grandmother out of a nursing home. The 'project' is an elaborate game instigated by one child to shame their parents into keeping her at home. It is only when the mother turns the tables, forcing the instigator to take over caring for the grandmother, that he realises what pressures his parents have been under for years. As so often in Anne Fine's novels, an entertainment turns into something else as a character is brought uncomfortably close to the nitty-gritty of real life.

There are other kinds of realisation. Will, the narrator of *The Book of the Banshee*, takes great pleasure in revealing how awful his sister is. Better still, he can let us know how awful everyone else in the family finds her, too: 'And our house is a battleground too, in its own way. That's what Mum says, at least. She claims that since Estelle turned into a shrieking banshee overnight, our house has been hell on earth' (p. 21).

This is from early in the novel; inevitably, Will has a few things to learn before the end. The most painful thing is not that, deep down, his sister turns out to be as human and caring as he is. Nor is it the painful realisation that he has been *letting* the house turn into a battleground ('I'm a coward'). It is that he, too, has been crashing through puberty, causing his parents as much stress as his sister: 'Both of them glowered at me. I glowered

back. I was just about to say, "Excuse me for living!" when I was inter-
rupted . . .' (p. 139). In fact, all this is a positive step. Will, awkward,
gangling, keep-your-mouth-shut Will, has found his voice. (In one of Anne
Fine's neat interweavings of the narrative, so has his tiny younger sister,
who has spent most of the novel as an elective mute.)

What helped him to find his voice? Telling the story, of course. In Will's
case, it is a kind of diary, the *book* of the Banshee. By the time he has
finished it, he has learned a lot – about other people, and about himself.

Parents are key players in these novels of family life. *Flour Babies* (1992),
the novel which brings a young character closest to the trials of parenthood, actually forces him into a parental role. A class of year 10 boys have
to become the rearers of imaginary children for several weeks. The joke in
the novel – and it is not really a joke, of course – is that big, lumbering
Simon really *is* bothered about the flour-sack infant. He realises, after talking
to his 'baby', almost pleading with the ridiculous object, that she has taken
over his life: 'He'd really grown to love his flour baby. He'd really cared
about her' (pp. 152–3). *That* is what parenthood is like, as many adult
readers would confirm. But Simon is not quite one of us yet, because 'she
wasn't real! And so he was free! Free, free, free!' (p. 153).

The ending of *Flour Babies* shows Anne Fine at her most wryly knowing,
and goes some way towards explaining why her novels are so popular with
teachers and librarians (i.e. adults). The flour babies belonging to the whole
class are just sitting there, and he kicks them all to pieces; they are just flour-
sacks, after all. He presents an amazing sight as he strides down the corridor
covered in flour. His teacher 'fell back respectfully to let the young vision
in white sail past, like a tall ship, out into his unfettered youth' (p. 156).

Unfettered. Not like us, eh? It's no wonder *Flour Babies* won the Carnegie
Medal *and* the Whitbread Award – they are in the gift of adults.

A few of Anne Fine's family novels for younger readers are worth
mentioning. In *Press Play* (1994), a mother has had the foresight to tape-
record all the instructions and reminders necessary to get her three children
(including a very young one) off to school. It is clever and witty – one of
her *jeux d'esprit* – but any young readers who take for granted the things
their parents do for them are brought right up against the realities. *Press
Play* was published only a couple of years after *Flour Babies*, and in many
ways it presents a pared-down exploration of the earlier book's themes.
Instead of three weeks' continuous child-care, the children in *Press Play*
have to manage only half-an-hour of a parent's lifelong routine. But it is
a start – and its ending is as clever, and as knowing, as that of *Flour Babies*.
In *Press Play*, the children close the kitchen door behind them after a hectic
half-hour or so:

> Then they turned to one another and said:
>   'Phew!'

Back in the kitchen, there was a silence as the tape ran on towards its end. Then, suddenly, the voice said:

'Phew!'

Then it fell silent.

(p. 34)

The Haunting of Pip Parker (1992), a picture-book, describes a little girl's fear of the skull-shaped glow on her bedroom wall. Her parents attempt to put her at her ease about it, or else they dismiss the idea entirely: it never seems to be there when *they* look. By the end of the book Pip has had to work out for herself what the glow is: a useful lesson in independence – and the fallibility of adult advice.

In *Countdown* (1996), a rather preachy short novel, parental guidance comes out more favourably: a father talks his son, Hugo, into experimenting with life as a caged animal – Hugo wants to keep a gerbil – and the boy is forced to realise how unbearable such a life would be. In *The Worst Child I Ever Had* (1991), the victory belongs to the child. Her 'crime' is very minor – she likes snails so much that she invites them into the house to watch television – but there is plenty of scope for discussion about what constitutes acceptable behaviour.

School life

Occasionally in Anne Fine's family novels, school is a convenient prop. Sometimes school serves as a useful 'framing device': the narrative in both *Goggle-Eyes* and *Step by Wicked Step*, as we have seen, is prompted by, in the former, an astute teacher and, in the latter, an administrative accident on a school trip which throws together children with similar experiences. In *The Granny Project*, school presents an opportunity for blackmail: the siblings' father is a teacher at their school, and the 'project' would make him a laughing-stock. Sometimes school simply helps the plot along: in *Madame Doubtfire* the children arrive home, inconveniently, because of industrial action by teachers – which puts the novel into a convenient historical context, I suppose.

But much of Anne Fine's fiction is based right *inside* schools, and these novels take seriously this formative territory in children's lives.

Two school-based novels for 'middle-range' reader (around ages 8–10) contain elements of fantasy. In *The Angel of Nitshill Road* (1992), a new girl, Celeste – *Celeste!* – seems to have been sent from heaven. In *Bill's New Frock* (1989), a boy becomes a girl for a day. As one might expect, these two novels are as serious as they are playful.

The Angel of Nitshill Road is about bullying. Barry Hunter has latched on to three misfits in his class, and he is making their lives a misery. When Celeste arrives, she does not cast a spell to magic their troubles away: she spends a long time helping the misfits to integrate more fully into the everyday life of the class. Angels do not have magic wands, but they do have *books*. About two-thirds of the way through the novel, Celeste uses a book to add the finishing touch to her good work: the involvement of the other pupils – and their teacher. A blank-paged book becomes a signed, witnessed account of all the nasty things Barry Hunter does; and, like all books, it has real power. When the teacher reads it, he is appalled; not because it is all news to him but because 'he'd known everything he needed all along. But . . . he had pretended not to see, not to hear, not to understand' (p. 86).

I do not think that Anne Fine has deliberately set out to present the teacher in a bad light. As I have already suggested, she is very aware that many of her readers are teachers, and it seems to me that in this novel she wants to say as much to them as to her younger readers. Why not spread the net wide, after all? Everyone in the school community is in this together, and adults need to be on the case as well. Although *The Angel of Nitshill Road* is not an earnest novel – it is full of word-games and jokes – there seems to be the force of real conviction behind it.

Bill's New Frock (1989) is another prizewinner. Published just two years after *Madame Doubtfire*, it, too, deals with a male character who changes his gender identity. Although written for a younger readership than the latter novel, its premiss is more daring: when he wakes up one schoolday morning, Bill really has become a girl.

Once given that narrative kick-start, *Bill's New Frock* seems to go effortlessly where it is going. At home, he is suddenly 'Poppet' – bad enough, but it is on his way to school that the implications of his new identity really start to make themselves felt. He is whistled at – *whistled at!* – by the boy who usually thumps him. He is patronised by the headteacher rather than being told off, as he usually is, for being late: '"Hurry along, dear, we don't want to miss assembly, do we?"' (p. 12).

Once inside the school building, Bill begins a miserable day. Girls, he discovers, have to be neat; girls, of course, are not allowed to do the hard physical jobs; even in the stories they read, girls are forced into a very narrow role: 'The Lovely Rapunzel didn't seem to *do* very much. She just got stolen out of spite by the witch . . .' (p. 19). Bill has to learn his new role quickly, and the entertainment comes from the ways in which he usually gets it wrong. The reader, of course, has to learn with him.

In fact, a lot of this does not seem very new at the start of the twenty-first century. Some of the points made in 1989 seem quite commonplace now – but that does not spoil the entertainment value of the bizarre narrative spin initiated on the first page. Moreover, almost any incident would provide material for discussion in class today: *are* girls still treated so differently from boys? (After all, it was written before most of its current readers were born.)

(Anne Fine takes a less than full-frontal approach to gender stereotyping in *The Same Story Every Year*, a 1992 easy reader for a younger audience.

In it, a primary-school teacher has to do the Nativity play, as usual. The teacher is fed up – it's the same story every year – but directs the play, sorts out the fights, knits a blanket for the baby Jesus. The teacher is a *man*.)

Stranger Danger? (1989) is a short novel – a short story, really – in a series for very young readers. It opens with the pupils in a class being taught one of the mantras of late twentieth-century life: Do not talk to strangers. Joe, the main character, goes out into the real world, and has to make decisions about what 'stranger' really means. He sometimes gets it wrong, and young readers can feel comfortable that they are at least as aware of the rules as Joe is. It is familiar territory for its intended audience, but it neatly illustrates how, in Anne Fine's novels, lessons in school – and lessons in *books* – become lessons for life. The reader is taken along with Joe, and is forced to make those tricky decisions with him.

The best do both at the same time

There is another theme which is common to many of Anne Fine's novels. I have already dealt with how she demonstrates – *advocates* – the power of stories. This section deals with the way she holds up for examination the nuts and bolts of storytelling and story-writing. Not, in other words, what the stories are about, but *how* they are told.

The book that celebrates more forcefully than any other the activity of writing is *The Book of the Banshee*. As well as dealing with the themes of adolescence and family relationships, already covered, the novel is *about* writing. It shows Anne Fine revelling in different narrative approaches and genres. There is a story within a story: Will is sustained by the autobiographical writings of a First World War soldier, William Saffery, and the way he relates Saffery's story to his own life is an object lesson in active reading. There is a visiting author (surely based on Anne Fine herself?) who is the one to prompt Will to write his own book. There is disguise: the visiting author is called Alicia Whitley, an author unknown to Will – until she explains that her pen-name is 'Alec Whitsun', Will's favourite author. There is further disguise in the closing paragraphs of *The Book of the Banshee*. Will takes a leaf out of Alicia Whitley's book, so to speak, and decides he needs a pen-name himself: he does not want anybody – especially Estelle, the banshee – to recognise his work when he gets it published. Anne Fine turns his musings into a *tour de force*:

> I'll choose a female name – a plain one so that no-one will even notice. I'll pick Anne. And since it's a pretty good book for someone my age ... I'll call myself Anne Good. No. Too prissy. Anne Best? Worse. Sounds too boastful. How about Anne Fine?

(p. 155)

This is great stuff. Anne Fine harks back to eighteenth-century novels, presented as the genuine writings of their narrators. At the same time, she plays postmodern games with the reader, foregrounding the artificiality of what she is doing. And if any reader fails to appreciate this outrageous bit of cheek, Anne Fine – or 'Anne Fine' – tops it. Will creates a title for his book out of the stuck-on gold letters of the old ledger he has been using: *The Beshoohoefte Bank* conveniently becomes *The Book of the Banshee*, 'the title I had in mind from the start', as he tells us. (In the library copy I was using to research this chapter, a previous reader had methodically crossed out all the letters of *The Beshoohoefte Bank* as though solving a cryptic crossword clue. As I said, Anne Fine likes games.)

Anne Fine has written books about writing for a 'middle-range' audience. *How to Write Really Badly* (1996) may sound like the title of an ironic instruction manual, but in fact is about the attitude of a new boy to the apparent incompetence of his desk partner. At first, the reader is taken aback by the new boy's rudeness and arrogance. By the end of the novel the new boy is helping his partner – and being helped by him – without really realising it. The title, of course, is as ironic as it sounds.

Jennifer's Diary (1996) is another novel in which a character who is good at writing looks down on someone who is not. Iolanthe is appalled that Jennifer has a diary when all she can think of to write in it is, for example, 'Jan 7th. Nothing much happened.' Iolanthe covets the diary, but Jennifer does not want her to have it. At first, Iolanthe merely adds to Jennifer's meagre entries, but that is of little use. What Iolanthe has to do is take Jennifer – and the reader – through the writing process. In the end, Jennifer is pleased to let her have the diary. Like *How to Write Really Badly*, *Jennifer's Diary* is about a maturing relationship.

We are back with lessons for life. In many Anne Fine novels, the act of putting down words on paper is central to the lessons the characters learn: the book in *The Angel of Nitshill Road*, the enforced neatness of Bill's writing in *Bill's New Frock*, the diaries Simon and his classmates have to keep in *Flour Babies*, all contribute to their understanding. And having them write things down is useful for Anne Fine on at least two levels. First, it illustrates how 'stories . . . help': we see the process and we see the results. Second, we see the growth that is taking place, in the characters' own words, before our very eyes. The importance of writing could not be more strongly foregrounded, putting it on the same level as story*telling* in some of her other novels. The delight that Anne Fine takes in the crafting of narrative has already been touched on. There are so many other ways in which her passion for writing is made evident that I can only begin to list them here.

She likes to explore the implications of different kinds of narrative. In the fantasy novels discussed, for instance, she gives us a kind of choice. In *The Angel of Nitshill Road*, you do not have to believe Celeste is an angel if you do not want to. The characters' doubts, Anne Fine's deliberate playing with figurative language, and the fact that, let us face it, the existence of angels is hardly self-evident, all allow the reader plenty of room to doubt. The doubt is part of the fun. One of the strengths of *Bill's New Frock* is the deadpan ordinariness of the narrative: *no one* bats an eyelid about the gender change, and the events are reported as real. But, boys do not just turn into girls, and there is a (slightly disappointing?) get-out clause if you want it: 'It's over. It's *over*. It doesn't matter if it was a dream, or not. *Whatever it was*, it's all over' (p. 96).

There are *narrators*. Many of Anne Fine's novels are written in the third person, but some of the more interesting have first-person narrators. We have seen how characters who tell stories – Will in *The Book of the Banshee*, Kitty in *Goggle-Eyes*, the serial narrators of *Step by Wicked Step* – all grow through the very narratives that they are relating. They are not exactly *unreliable* as narrators, but they have had to move a long way from their original positions by the time they are presenting a more rounded picture at the end. (A contrast can be made with a short book for younger readers, *Diary of a Killer Cat* (1994). We cannot believe anything this narrator tells us, and it would make a marvellous introduction to the device of the first-person narrator and point of view.)

Names are always important in her novels. The most daring name-change is that of Daniel in *Madame Doubtfire*. He takes the idea of the pseudonym a step beyond what Will does in *The Book of the Banshee*: his new name goes with an entirely new identity, and it is a neat irony that his wife learns of his true feelings only through this re-writing of himself. In *Bill's New Frock*, that other exploration of gender identity, Bill never actually gets a new name. If he is addressed as anything, it is 'Poppet' or 'dear' – fertile ground for any class discussion on gender. Bill is allowed to retain his identity for the reader (he is always 'Bill' in the narrative), but he is not allowed any individual identity as a girl – and *that*, according to the novel, is often how it is.

Sometimes, people are careless with names. In *Flour Babies*, there are ridiculous scenes in which Martin Simon, the school boffin, and Simon Martin, the novel's lumbering, underachieving hero, are placed in the wrong sets by an administrative error. In *How to Write Really Badly* the new boy is so exasperated by his new teacher's inability to understand that he is Chester Howard, not Howard Chester, that he gives up. The importance of names helps to emphasise the resolution he reaches, described in the closing paragraphs of the novel: 'I ought to tell Miss Tate my real name some time, I suppose. . . . Then again, maybe I won't. Howard is *nicer* than Chester, after all. And, when you think about it, Howard's *happier*' (p. 112). In other words, these are more than mere games that Anne Fine is playing.

Then there are the nicknames. The titles of two of her most ambitious books, *The Book of the Banshee* and *Goggle-Eyes*, are based on nicknames.

Both books explore how the narrators who invented the names come to an understanding about the victims of their name-calling. In *The Angel of Nitshill Road*, nicknames are some of the things which make the three misfits so unhappy. It is another of Anne Fine's lessons for life: how we refer to other people – and how we encourage them to think about themselves – is of key importance to the relationships they have with us, and with the world.

These are big narrative themes, treated seriously. But it is interesting to notice that we have come down to the very building-blocks of the story-teller's trade: words. Anne Fine loves words, and she loves to play with them. There are punning titles: *Step By Wicked Step* is not a horror novel but a portmanteau of stories about step-parents; *The Same Story Every Year* refers both to the Nativity story itself and to the same old story that the long-suffering teacher is instructed by his headmistress to stage, year after year, accompanied by the assurance that this *will* be the last year he will have to do it. The visiting writer in *The Book of the Banshee* deliberately refers to the pupils in the year 3 classes she has to entertain – 3B and 3P – as 'threebies' and 'threepies'. (Since reading the book, I have thought of liberating a restless class of mine, 10B3. Free the 'Tenby Three'.) In *The Angel of Nitshill Road* there are many teasing verbal clues, in addition to her name, that Celeste is an angel: she smiles 'seraphically' (long word, that, in a book for middle-range readers); she has dropped in 'out of the blue'; her father could not stay because he 'had to fly'. The teacher is presented with plenty of playful opportunities to explore with children the dangers of taking figurative language too literally. Nor are the clues lost on the characters: they have to puzzle out, at the same time as the reader, whether Celeste really is an angel.

This is the all-important link: the reader is always *there*, working out the 'doggy business' of life along with the characters. Anne Fine's novels take readers to some interesting places – but by the time we are ready to return, we usually bring something back with us.

References

Works by Anne Fine referred to in this chapter:
(1983) *The Granny Project*, London: Methuen.
(1987) *Madame Doubtfire*, London: Penguin.
(1989) *Bill's New Frock*, London: Methuen Mammoth.
—— *Goggle-Eyes*, London: Puffin.
—— *Stranger Danger?*, London: Hamish Hamilton.
(1991) *The Book of the Banshee*, London: Hamish Hamilton.
—— *The Worst Child I Ever Had*, London: Puffin.
(1992) *The Angel of Nitshill Road*, London: Methuen.
—— *Flour Babies*, London: Hamish Hamilton.
—— *The Haunting of Pip Parker*, London: Walker Books.

—— *The Same Story Every Year*, London: Hamish Hamilton Gazelles.
(1994) *Diary of a Killer Cat*, London: Puffin.
—— *Press Play*, London: Piccadilly Press.
(1995) *Step by Wicked Step*, London: Puffin.
(1996) *Countdown*, London: Heinemann Banana Books.
—— *How to Write Really Badly*, London: Methuen.
—— *Jennifer's Diary*, London: Hamish Hamilton Antelopes.

POSTSCRIPT

From time to time, almost everyone finds themselves asking, 'Am I leading the right life? Is this really how I ought to be spending my one life on the planet?' But it is strange to read a study of your work over a twenty-five-year period, and realise, for the very first time, that this question is one you have been asking and answering over and over in your books.

I look back at particular novels, and I see one piece of work that proved awkward or demanding, emotionally or technically; or another that proved to be almost a pleasure to write from start to finish – what Simon in *Flour Babies* would have called 'a good laugh'. I reread some text, and remember how easily this section came, or how hard it was to find a way through that particular thicket of plot. I recall the satisfying triumph of weaving one last joke into that chapter, or recognise I must have approached this section with the author's notorious sliver of ice in the heart: 'Oh, brilliant! *That* will make 'em cry!' I see books even through the veil of what was happening when I was working on them: the year after we separated; the months we had the builders in; the summer all four children at once were taking important exams.

But I would never see an overall pattern. I know that there are things I do as a matter of course, or of conviction, in my books: offer my readers the vision of caring men and determined, working women; show men who shop and cook regularly, not just to impress guests on a Saturday night; highlight the civilised, co-operative side of schools – especially since television has left too many viewers, young and old, with the impression that pushy grunting in our classrooms and playgrounds is acceptable behaviour, when it certainly is not. (It is more a matter of time: with strict limits to the hours child actors may work there is no time for mistakes, so it is safer to write a six-word interchange – 'Lend us yer book.' 'Nah.' 'Gissit!' – than to invite the number of takes necessary for a more normal, lengthy and amiable interchange.) I try to show children as I think they are. Why should I think mine are the only keen-eyed, critical, sensitive, compassionate young people on the planet? And I do not shy away from thinking about moral or socio-political issues because I both write slowly and get bored fast. If what I am writing does not keep my interest, it certainly will not keep that of the reader. So, the more layers to each book the better – especially since I believe that the novel still is, and always will be, the very best instrument we have for ethical enquiry.

But it is strange to peek over someone's shoulder and see your work as another sees it. Jim Jones' observations came as a bit of a shock. Do I do that? I suppose I do. Is that really what I think? Yes, I suppose it is. Do I think that it is so important? Yes, I do.

The book is the person, so they say. So we would expect him to be pretty accurate. (He seems to have read *everything*.) But what I really had not realised is how much the sheer intrinsic value of the written word shows through the novels. I thought (particularly in this year of being 50) I had only just begun to wonder if locking myself away in absolute silence for months on end is really the way I want to live my life. (Alan Sillitoe cannot have been the first to point out that an author has to choose between writing and living.) But what is made clear by Jim Jones' study is that the value of writing is something I've been querying all along, in different ways, book after book.

And it is a great comfort to be reminded that the answer I have come to consistently, through so many of my characters, is: Yes. It *is* worth it. Carry on.

Anne Fine

Index